AF566889

PUBLIC SECTOR ROAD TRANSPORT CORPORATION

A COMPARATIVE STUDY WITH PRIVATE SECTOR

PUBLIC SECTOR ROAD TRANSPORT CORPORATION

A COMPARATIVE STUDY WITH PRIVATE SECTOR

G. JOHN GUNASEELAN
P.G. Department of Commerce,
Voorhees College, Vellore

Foreword by

DR. DEBENDRA KUMAR DAS
Professor, University Department of Economics,
B.R.A. Bihar University, Muzaffarpur

DEEP & DEEP PUBLICATIONS
F-159, Rajouri Garden, New Delhi-110027

ISBN 81-7629-081-5

© 1998 G. JOHN GUNASEELAN

All rights reserved with the Publisher, including the right to translate
or to reproduce this book or parts thereof except for
brief quotations in critical articles or reviews.

Typeset by ASHISH TECHNOGRAPHICS, 3190, Mohindra Park, Shakur Basti,
Delhi-110034.

Printed in India at ELEGANT PRINTERS, A 38/2, Maya Puri,
Phase-I, New Delhi-110064.

Published by DEEP & DEEP PUBLICATIONS, F-159, Rajouri Garden,
New Delhi-110027. Phones : 5435369, 5440916

Dedicated to:
My Parents
Capt. D. Gnana Rathnam
and
Mrs. Daisy Vijayavathi

Contents

Foreword

State Transport Undertakings (STUs) were established as bus transport operators in public sector over the last four decades. It is proved beyond doubt that for the developed States like Tamil Nadu, Maharashtra, Andhra Pradesh, Gujarat, Karnataka, Haryana and Punjab, STUs played a significant role in their overall development.

Over the years, the STUs have developed certain strengths—availability of bus fleet, infrastructure for maintenance of buses, technical knowhow, operational knowhow, trained staff, organised system and financial support. But in recent decades, STUs were losing their ground, and at the same time, their customer's share. Today, the customers have different alternatives and options for travel mode. The private operators offer stiff competition wherever possible.

In order to constantly add value to the transport service and contemplate strategic action, public transport corporations need to stay close to the travelling passenger. It is therefore, essential to establish a system that transmits customer feed back to transport management periodically and in time to enable prompt corrective action wherever necessary. Hence, the importance of the concept of "user satisfaction" and its vital role in ensuring better quality of service in bus operations.

Dr. G. John Gunaseelan has done a significant comparative research study of passenger satisfaction in public bus transport corporation with private bus operations in North Arcot Region, Tamil Nadu. The study reveals that the passengers are satisfied with the operation of buses by public and private sector in North Arcot Region. However, the passengers are relatively more satisfied with public sector bus operation, namely, Pattukottai Azagiri Transport Corporation (PATC) than the private sector operation. The author concludes that the STUs may play a high profile in the case of long route services and the private operators in short route services.

I congratulate the author for focussing on an important debatable area in public bus transport system, i.e., passenger satisfaction and suggesting a package of proposals to improve the service-oriented transport operations. I hope the teachers, transport management experts, transport economists, researchers and policy-makers would find the findings of the study useful and stimulating.

Muzaffarpur DEBENDRA KUMAR DAS

Preface

Nationalised bus passenger road transport in India is more than four decade old. The issue of nationalisation is, however, still debatable. In recent years there has been a lot of discussion over the privatisation of the transport sector. The share of passenger road transport in the hands of State Transport Undertakings (STUs), measured in term of fleet strength in the public sector, has progressively declined from 45 per cent in 1980-81, to 34 per cent in 1989-90. According to the National Transport Policy Committee "future nationalisation should be guided by efficiency of operation of existing undertaking and the extent to which they can provide consumer satisfaction. . ."

Apart from the financial performance, the passenger amenities and benefits have a greater stake in deciding the mix between the private and public transport operators. Where amenities and comforts for passengers increase preference for such operations may also increase. Consequently it may pave the way for higher share for STUs or private operators. Hence there is a need to know the opinion of the passengers as to their preference for a particular transport system, and the level of travel of satisfaction. The result of such a survey would be of immense help to the policy-makers in government and other authorities in evolving a proper transport policy.

The present book gives a comparative passengers' satisfaction between the operation of a State Transport Corporation, viz., PATC in Tamil Nadu and private bus sector, besides, physical and financial performance evaluation of PATC. The study involves collection of primary and secondary data.

The secondary data were collected from published records such as performance statistics of STUs published by Central Institute of Road Transport, (Pune), Annual report of PATC, Government reports and published books and journal to review the performance of STUs in India, Tamil Nadu and PATC. The primary data for the study were collected through personal interview of the passenger respondents.

I am grateful to many persons for their invaluable contribution in the completion of this time consuming work. First, I wish to record my deep sense of gratitude to my guide Dr. S. Shanmugasundaram, Professor and Head of the Department of Commerce, Madras University P.G. Extension Centre, Salem. It has been a rewarding experience to work under his supervision and I find no words to express my gratitude adequately for all the trouble he has undertaken in the direction and preparation of this book. I am grateful to the authorities of the University of Madras for having awarded me the Ph.D. Degree on the basis of this study and also for having permitted me to publish the book.

I am indebted to Dr. P. Jegadish Gandhi, Professor of Economics, Voorhees College, Vellore, who had been a source of inspiration to undertake research in the area of transport. I am fortunate to have academic association with him all these years. I grateful to Dr. R. Jayakaran Issac, Principal, Voorhees College and Prof. Dr. K.V. Viswanathan, former Commerce Prof. and Head, Annamalai University for their encouragement and support in my academic endeavours. I thank my colleagues Dr. M. Anbalagan, Mr. Arulappan, Mr. Thiyagukumar for their active support in my academic endeavours.

I am thankful to Dr. Debendra Kumar Das, University Department of Economics, B.R.A. Bihar University, Muzaffarpur, who at my request has gone through the manuscript meticulously and has given a valuable 'Foreword'. I am highly beholden to him. In a special way, I thank Deep & Deep Publications, New Delhi for bringing out this publication in a record time.

Vellore G. JOHN GUNASEELAN

Abbreviations

ASRTUs	Association of State Road Transport Undertakings
ASS	Average Satisfaction Score
ASTC	Annai Satya Transport Corporation Limited
ATC	Anna Transport Corporation Limited
CIRT	Central Institute of Road Transport
CPKM	Cost Per Kilometre
CRC	Cholan Roadways Corporation Limited
CTC	Cheran Transport Corporation Limited
DCTC	Dheeran Chinnamalai Transport Corporation Limited
DEA	Data Envelopment Analysis
DEI	Data Envelopment Index
EPKM	Earnings per Kilometre
MGRTC	M.G. Ramachandran Transport Corporation Limited
JTC	Jeeva Transport Corporation Limited
KMPL	Kilometre run per Litre of Diesel
KTC	Kattabomman Transport Corporation Limited
MPTC	Marudhu Pandiyar Transport Corporation Limited
NTC	Nesamony Transport Corporation Limited
OR	Occupancy Ratio
PATC	Pattukottai Azhagiri Transport Corporation Limited
PRC	Pandian Roadways Corporation Limited
PS	Passenger Satisfaction
PSI	Passenger Satisfaction Index
PSS	Passenger Satisfaction Score
PTC	Pallavan Transport Corporation Limited
RMTC	Rani Mangammal Transport Corporation Limited
SRTU	State Road Transport Undertaking

STC	State Transport Corporation
STU	State Transport Undertaking
TNSTCs	Tamil Nadu State Transport Corporations
TNSTUs	Tamil Nadu State Transport Undertakings
TPTC	Thanthai Periyar Transport Corporation Limited
TTC	Thiruvalluvar Transport Corporation Limited
VMR	Vehicle-Man Ratio

1

Introduction

1. INTRODUCTION

Transport is an important infrastructure in the economy of any country. Transport assumes a greater role in developing countries since all the sectors of the development are closely dependent upon the existence of suitable transportation network. The transport sector which undertakes movement of people and goods from one place to another constitutes one of the most important sectors in the present world. It is a part of daily life having all enveloping influence on every one of us. There is no individual today who is not directly or indirectly served by public transport. In fact, the whole structure of industry and commerce rests on the well laid foundation of transportation. Thus an effective transport system is a prerequisite for economic development.

Of all the types of transport, passenger transport has been acclaimed as the most important. Today, it has become the principal means of moving people both in rural and urban areas. Places have been brought nearer to one another, breaking their isolation which was a characteristic feature of the olden days when this particular mode of transport was not available. In India, bus transport is cheap and easily available and it is the common man's mode of transport.

2. NATIONALISATION OF ROAD TRANSPORT

Passenger Road Transport is a public utility service and as such it is the duty of a welfare state to provide the most economical and comfortable service to the public. By enacting the Road Transport Corporation Act, the Government of India recognised, as far back as in 1950, the fact that provision of passenger bus service was more desirable in the public sector than in the private sector and committed itself to a policy of nationalisation of the passenger transport services. The following are the factors that prompted the nationalisation of the transport sector:[1]

It is a public utility service having social obligation.

It is a labour-intensive venture having potential to generate employment.

It is a source of revenue for the Government.

It has capacity to yield return on investment.

It provides infrastructure for overall development by accelerating the economic activities.

State ownership is a powerful method of brining about co-ordination in the management of the transportation network, for, it brings the various modes of transport into a system, which facilitates the implementation of a unified transport policy. The state is in a position to make rational estimates of demand and supply of transport facilities by model choice, and to provide more comprehensive and efficient transport service. Most of the States/Union Territories have nationalised passenger transport in varying degrees and 68 State Road Transport Corporations (SRTCs) were operating in the country, owning 34.2 per cent of the total buses and carrying 5.96 crores of passengers per day on an average in 1989-90.[2]

3. STATE TRANSPORT UNDERTAKINGS

The Tamil Nadu Government's policy of nationalising the passenger transport service was launched in Madras City in October 1947. Stage by stage, by July 1948 the entire service in the Madras city was nationalised. During 1956, after the re-organisation of the States, services already nationalised in Kanyakumari District came under the State Transport Department. The first long distance express bus service was started in August 1959 based on the policy that all routes exceeding 120 miles should be exclusively operated by the Department with express services and several long distance routes were opened from time to time. In 1971, the policy of nationalising passenger transport gained further momentum with the formation of four state corporations owned by Government of Tamil Nadu, namely, Pallavan, Cheran, Cholan and Pandiyan in different regions of the state.

With progressive nationalisation and bifurcation of the bigger units and the establishment of new corporations the number of Transport Corporations has increased to 16 in Tamil Nadu at present. Some corporations like Pallavan, Cheran, Pandiyan, Cholan, Kattabomman, Marudhu Pandiyar, Deeran Chinnamalai and Rani Mangammal were named after famous ancient rulers in Tamil Nadu and others, Pattukottai Azhagiri, Anna, Thanthai Periyar, Jeeva, Nesamony and M.G.R. Corporations were named after the leaders of political parties while the Thiruvalluvar Corporation was named after the great Tamil poet. Annai Sathya Transport Corporation was named after the late mother of the then Chief Minister of Tamil Nadu. In Tamil Nadu out of 8,245 passenger vehicles the State Corporations owned 1,975 which accounted for 24 per cent in 1969-70. In the year 1989-90 the share of the public sector increased to 70 per cent of the total fleet of 16,829 passenger vehicles. 15 Transport Corporations together were operating 12,019 buses on 9,895 routes in that year, carrying every day nearly 128 lakh passengers over 45 lakh kms and employing 1,00,500 persons.[3] Thus the Public Passenger Road Transport Sector has come to stay in Tamil Nadu and is poised for an unprecedented growth in future.

4. ROLE OF PRIVATE SECTOR IN PASSENGER TRANSPORTATION

Private sector too equally plays a vital role in passenger transportation. They account for more than 60 per cent of total number of buses in India and 30 per cent in Tamil Nadu. Profit motive is the prime motive of any business establishment and the private bus operators are no exception to this. They are being criticised for making abnormal profit by indulging in unfair practices such as overloading, deviating from the regular routes, not going up to the destination and indulging in unhealthy competition among themselves as well as with the public sector buses. At the same time they are also noted for their personalised service to the passengers, which is reflected in concessions to the regular travellers, not claiming fare for children and entertaining passengers with luggage. Thus both public and private sectors are contributing to the development of passenger transport in their own way.

5. STUDIES ON PUBLIC SECTOR TRANSPORT

The author has come across a number of books, articles, reports and studies. A brief review of which is given below under four headings.

1. Evaluation Parameters

Murthy, S.S. in his study "Criteria for Evaluation of STUs" has highlighted the limitations of the conventional parameters of evaluating the performance of STUs and suggested a new methodology known as 'Capital Recovery Index' which emphasises the ability of STUs to generate cash and recoupment of investment.[4]

Bagade, M.V. in his study entitled "A New Look at Performance Appraisal of STUs" has evolved two types of methodology for evaluation of STUs. One is known as Quality of Service Index (QSI), designed to measure the effectiveness of the quality of operation. It is a weighted index computed by assigning appropriate weights for the responses of the passenger relating to safety, reliability, punctuality and regularity of operations. The same methodology has been followed in this thesis. The second is known as 'Data Envelopment Analysis', which aims to measure the overall productivity of STUs, in terms of Input made and Output produced. It is widely accepted by transport economists.[5]

Hanumantha Rao Ch. in his paper "Comparative study of certain Traffic Parameters in selected STUs" has evaluated the performance of the major STUs in India using certain selected traffic parameters such as Vehicle utilisation, Crew utilisation and Occupation ratio.[6]

Patankar, P.G. in his study "Quality in Road Passenger Transportation" has emphasised the quality in service sector, especially road transport. He has prescribed certain parameters to judge the quality of service offered by the transport undertaking such as, punctuality, reliability, passenger amenities and comfort, incidence of breakdowns, accidents and nature and quantum of public complaints. He has concluded with an appeal to the STUs to uphold the motto of 'Service to Travellers'.[7]

Anand Swaroop Behara in his paper on "Methodologies for Augmentation of Bus Services on existing Routes in STUs" has suggested two models to work out augmentation of buses in STUs—one based on adequacy criteria and the other on breakdown concept and argues that a balance has to be achieved between the two while finalising the plans of augmentation.[8]

Deshmukh, A.R. in his paper on "Creative Accounting: A New Social Cost Benefits Approach to Read the Balance Sheets of STUs: A case of MSRTC" has reiterated the unfavourable factors responsible for the mounting losses of STUs and viewed that the present accounting policies in STUs are not proper. He has argued that the STUs are working against many odds and therefore, if some of the present accounts policies followed by them are reversed, it can result in a much-needed turn around from loss-making to profit-making.[9]

2. Issues in Public Passenger Road Transport

Sundarsanam Padam in his paper on "Nationalisation of Passenger Road Transport—Looking Back and Looking Forward" has traced back the historical account of STUs and the circumstances under which it has been brought forth, so as to illustrate that public sector has been introduced into bus transport industry due to the inability of the private sector to operate efficient and adequate services and to provide social welfare. He has also cautioned that any attempt to revive private sector would bring back the deficiency of private sector operation.[10]

Mahesh Chand in his study "Current Issues in Public Road Transport Management", has made an attempt to evaluate critically the pros and cons of nationalisation, as well as the constraints of public transport management. He has highlighted its advantages to the economy and society at large and emphasised that nationalisation of passenger road transport should be given a strong momentum to complete the process of the nationalisation at the earliest.[11]

Devasahayam in his study on "State Transport-Making Undertakings Profitable" has pointed out that the SRTUs, can be converted into profitable instruments if only the management is oriented towards a culture of cost effectiveness. There should be more dialogue and better communication among States and between States and the Centre on this subject. The Association of State Road Transport Undertakings, which is the apex body of all the SRTUs can be activised to play a more effective and meaningful role in this respect.[12]

David Maunder *et. al.*, of the Overseas Unit of the Transport and Road Research Laboratory (TRRL) of UK in their study on "Matching Supply and Demand in India's Public Transport" have brought out the present scenario of passenger road transport operations in Indian cities at macro-level, as well as a detailed study on the operations of Delhi Transport Corporation. They also studied the travellers' options between conventional stage carriage buses and paratransit or Intermediate Public Transport modes (IPT) which include mini buses, tongas (horse-drawn carts) and all forms of rickshaws (cycle, auto and motor cycle) in three cities viz., Vadodara, Patna and Jaipur. They concluded that, by and large, urban public transport in India performs well given the limitations of resources available.[13]

Raghunathan V. *et al.*, have undertaken a study on behalf of ASRTUs on "Passenger Transport in India—A Customers' Perspective" and observed that the task performed by the STUs, given the socio-economic and environmental conditions is commendable and also felt that still there is room for improvement and suggested certain areas in which STUs have to improve their performance.[14]

Arora, S.K. in his book "Economics of Management in Road Transport Industry" has focussed on the problems of management in the road transport industry in general and suggested various techniques for evaluation of STUs, besides he had made a comparative performance evaluation of privately managed Road Transport Industry *vis-a-vis* state managed Industry in Punjab state and concluded that both the public sector undertakings—Punjab Roadways and Pepsu Road Transport Corporation—are operating much beyond their equilibrium levels and any further sanctioning of routes to them will only increase losses rather than yield profits. Only the private operators are operating below the equilibrium level and there is a scope for increasing their capacity utilisation and hence returns.[15]

Ratan Kumar Singh in his book "Road Transport and Economic Development" has evaluated the critical role played by road transport as a basic infrastructure in economic development and analysed the correlation between the development of road transport and that of other vital sectors of the economy in relation to Bihar State. He has studied the Bihar State Road Transport Corporation as a case and suggested certain guidelines for a suitable road development policy for Bihar and steps to be taken to improve the working and performance of the Bihar State Road Transport Corporation.[16]

Subrahmanyam, P. in his book "Organisational set-up of Road Transport" has made a comparative study of Andhra Pradesh State Road Transport Corporation with Road Transport Corporations in other States and suggested organisational measures needed to revitalize the road transport services in Andhra Pradesh to combat the problem of increasing losses.[17]

Santosh Sharma in his book "Productivity in Road Transport" has identified the critical factors which lead to economies and diseconomies in bus operation and presented a comprehensive approach in designing optimal operating systems through efficient planning in operational as well as functional areas.[18]

Alan Armstrong-Wright and Thiriz Sebastian in their study for the World Bank entitled "Bus Services—Reducing Costs, Raising Standards" have examined the nature, quantity and quality of bus services in cities of developing countries, which include the ownership of bus services and the variety of vehicles and the services, as well as co-operation and competition and their impact on viability and standards. The report also includes a set of performance indicators, with desirable level of performance, to measure and monitor the performance and quality of urban bus services.[19]

Ossewaarde, J.M. in his paper "Public Transport—Future Perspectives" has concluded that public transport no longer lives for the purpose of financial gains but for bringing about significant gains in public interest and well-being.[20]

Raman, A.V. in his paper "The Rationale of Nationalisation of Passenger Road Transport", has outlined the socio-economic and political advantages of STUs compared with that of private bus operators.[21]

Bagade in his paper "What ails State Transport" has discussed the external environment and government policy which have had a cumulative effect on the adverse financial viability of the STUs and stated that the road transport is an important infrastructure for development of the nation and is to be left more and more with the government than in the hands of private operators.[22]

Hanumantha Rao Ch. in his paper "Nationalised Passenger Road Transport in India—A Perspective" has discussed the role of STUs as a public enterprise and stated that the STUs should have long-term perspective plans in the changing context of policy prescription. His recommendations include, diagnostic studies for major loss-making STUs, commissioning of study projects on comparative transport operations in private *vs*. Public Sector.[23]

Raman, A.V. in his paper on "Case Against Privatisation" has brought out the manifold advantage of nationalising passenger road transport. The social and political advantages far outweigh the argument for the role of the private sector. Also the benefits of economy of scale, operational efficiency, passenger benefits and employees' welfare would accrue more tangibly in the public sector than in the private sector. The only argument against public sector road transport is its financial performance. Here, too, many external factors such as non-reimbursement of social costs, administratively fixed fare structures, are the causes rather than any deficiency of management.[24]

Vijaya Kumar K.C. in his paper on "Operating cost of Public Sector Transport Undertaking in India" has developed prediction estimation and assessed the contribution of each item of operating cost to the total cost. He concluded that when kilometer run increases, cost also increases except depreciation, cost on personnel and interest on capital.[25]

Kulshrestha, D.K. in his book on "Management of State Road Transports in India" has dealt with various managerial problems of State Road Transport Undertakings in the country and suggested measures to lower down the cost of bus operation as well as to improve the present level of income of the operators.[26]

Panduranga Rao has edited a book on "Dimensions of Rural Transportation" which is based on the deliberations of an International Seminar held in 1988 at Visakhapatnam. The book contains thirty contributions of experts, divided into four themes: (i) Role of Transport in the strategy for Rural Development; (ii) Rural Transport Scenario in India and abroad; (iii) Energy, Technology adoption, Safety and Environmental aspects of Rural Transport; and (iv) Rural Road Network Planning and Development.[27]

Patankar, P.G. in his book on "Road Passenger Transport in India", has presented his views on the nationalised bus transport sector, identified the problems besetting this sector and suggested appropriate solutions.[28]

Sudarsanam Padam in his book on "Bus Transport in India —the Structure, Management and Performance of Road Transport Corporations" has examined the impact of the organisation structure of the selected Road Transport Corporations on their performance and suggested suitable modifications in their structure so as to improve their performance.[29]

3. Case Studies

Parmar, B.D. in his study entitled "GSRTC performance: Remedy to recover losses" has studied the performance of Gujarat State Road Transport Corporation from the year of its inception (1960) to 1985-86 and stated that GSRTC's performance is satisfactory as far as infrastructure and public utility service are concerned. However, as a commercial venture it is a drain on the limited resources of the state because of huge losses and suggested the differential pricing and effective management to achieve the optimum efficiency and productivity so as to make up the losses.[30]

Sriramulu, C.T., *et. al*, in their paper on "`V' and `J' Service: A new concept in Urban Transit in Madras" have studied the efficiency of the `V' (Limited Stop Service) service and `J' (Selected Stop Service) service introduced by the Pallavan Transport Corporation, in Madras city.[31]

Rajeswar Rao in his study on "Management Effectiveness in Transport Operations—A Case Study of Delhi Transport Corporation" has made an attempt to study the management efficiency and effectiveness in managing the affairs of Delhi Transport Corporation (DTC). According to him, DTC in the public sector appeared to have suffered severe setback due to management's ineffectiveness in most of the important functional areas, and this had led to heavy and mounting losses and the consequent capital erosion. The author has suggested that the Delhi Transport Corporation immediately needs greater Governmental support and control, scientific organisational infrastructure, effective mechanism for planning and control of traffic operations, efficient engineering and fleet maintenance services, sound financial management practices and optimum use of the available resources, viz., men, materials and fleet.[32]

Rajesh Chandra in his study on the "Financial Performance of Delhi Transport Corporation: A Social Accounting Approach" has analysed the performance of the Delhi Transport Corporation in financial terms as also in the context of social and economic benefits provided by it to specific sections of population such as students and physically handicapped in Delhi and suggested that the revenue loss resulting from such benefits should not be treated as financial loss.[33]

Dilip Kumar Halder in his study "Public Undertaking in Motor Bus Transportation in the city of Calcutta: An Economic Analysis and Programming Solutions" has assessed the performance of the Calcutta State Transport Corporation in general and with particular reference to the private operations in Calcutta and offered suggestions to CSTC in the areas of scheduling of vehicle, management of labour, maintenance of the fleet and development of a team of experts with the Corporation.

Bagade, M.V. in his study "Management Information System for passenger Bus Transport Industry (A Special Study of Maharashtra State Road Transport Corporation)" has designed MIS for transport industries, taking into consideration the three management levels, Top or Corporate Management, Middle or Executive Management and the Operating Management level, with a focus on MSRTC as a case.[35]

Dixit, M.C. in his study, "A Study of the Poona Municipal Transport Administration with reference to its Service Efficiency from 1959 onwards", has studied the cost, revenue and operational efficiency, as well as the pricing policy of the PMTC. Besides, a consumer opinions survey with regard to its performance has also been undertaken.[36]

Jegadish Gandhi in his paper "State Transport Undertakings in Southern States—A Comparative Study" has presented a comparative performance analysis of public road passenger transport system in Southern States, viz., Andhra, Karnataka, Kerala and Tamil Nadu.[37]

Kulkarni, S.D. in his study entitled, "Working and Problems of Passenger Road Transport in Maharashtra", has studied the working of public passenger road transportation in Maharashtra State and discussed the problems in the light of future growth of MSRTC.[38]

Daindas J. in his edited book on "Private Bus Transport in Sri Lanka—Its Performance, Productivity and Manpower" has studied in Operation of Private Omnibus Transport Industry in Sri Lanka, with special reference to the people who work in it. It mainly focuses on the working environment of the crew members as well as their socio-economic background.[39]

Thalavai Pillai in his research study entitled "Transport Corporations in Tamil Nadu—A Study of Performance of Pandiyan Roadways Corporation Ltd. and Cholan Roadways Corporation Ltd.", had made a comparative evaluation of the performance of the two state owned Transport Corporations of Tamil Nadu, namely, Pandian Roadways Corporation Ltd. and Cholan Corporation Ltd. Apart from evaluation of physical, financial and social performance, the opinion of the bus users as well as the employees toward the working of the respective Corporations had also been dealt with.[40]

4. Public and Private Bus Sectors—Compared

Charles Feibel and Walters, A.A. have undertaken a research project for the World Bank on "Ownership and Efficiency in Urban Buses" with the purpose of comparing the cost of services of privately owned buses with that of nationalised companies in three cities of developing countries, viz., Calcutta, Bangkok and Istanbul. One of their significant findings is that the private operators are able to ply their services at only 50 to 60 per cent of the cost of running the same service by government owned concerns. It is also observed that the quality of private bus services is not markedly inferior and usually superior to the public bus operators.[41]

Carapetis S. *et al*, in their study conducted for World Bank on "The Supply and Quality of Rural Transport Services in Developing Countries—A Comparative Review" have identified, reviewed and analysed various factors that influence the supply and quality of transport services in rural areas of developing countries. The data collected for the study were based on a series of short field surveys in India, Indonesia, Philippines, Srilanka, Sierra Leone and Tunisia during 1981 and the first half of 1982. The study has revealed the need for new perspectives in planning rural transport investment which require a better understanding of the real transport needs and problems of small farmers. These needs are often for personal travel and for moving small loads over relatively short distances.[42]

Walters, A.A. in his research report "Cost and Scale of Bus Services" has challenged the conventional belief that large buses in large organisations are the best arrangement to produce optimum frequencies in urban road passenger transport. He has surveyed a number of cities in developing countries (Philippines, Malaysia, Thailand and Argentina), where there is some freedom for private operators to enter the industry and observed that minibus services are often appropriate, giving the best frequencies and speed and suitably low average waiting time. He has also observed that throughout the cities surveyed, the municipal or nationalised bus concerns always have higher costs and concluded that the best institutional organisation is not the large firm but the small firm, often the owner/driver.[43]

David A. Hensher in his study on "Productive efficiency and ownership of urban bus services" has investigated the productivity differences between public and private bus service in Australia and stated that private supply of public passenger transport in general has performed more efficiently than public supply.[44]

Charles Downs in his study "Private and Public Local Bus Compared: The case of New York City" has compared private and public provision of local bus service in New York city. He observed that there is difference between the cost effectiveness of both operations and the differences are associated with differences in the scales of the organisations involved.[45]

Umrigar, F.S. *et al.*, in their paper entitled "Exploring the scope of private participation for urban public transport supply in India" have explored the bus operations in India and observed that for better efficiency and a higher level of service, healthy competition through private participation is desirable. They have suggested that an appropriate regulatory framework is required for a co-operative public-private mixed operation. While the public agency should co-ordinate the operation, private operators should also be consulted for planning the system.[46]

Dutta, P. in his paper "Private Bus Options" has suggested the induction of Private buses to meet the ever increasing demand for passenger transport and advocated three options by which private transport buses can be inducted. However, he is of the opinion that government should have the ultimate control on the overall bus transport options.[47]

6. THE PROBLEM

Nationalised bus passenger road transport in India is about four decades old. The issue of nationalisation is however, still controversial. On the one hand the STUs have been applauded for their social considerations and on the other they are vehemently criticised for their heavy losses year after year, inspite of their vantage position of a limited monopolistic nature and the benefits accruing from such a position such as economies of scale and professional management.

In recent years there has been a lot of talk over the privatisation of the transport sector. The share of passenger road transport in the hands of STUs, measured in terms of fleet strength in the public sector, has progressively declined. From 45.2 per cent (69,498) in 1980-81, it came down to 34.2 per cent (1,02,067) in 1989-90.[48] According to the National Transport Policy Committee (1980), "future nationalisation should be guided by efficiency of operation of existing undertakings and the extent to which they can provide consumer satisfaction. . ."[49] Apart from the financial performance, the passenger amenities and benefits have a greater stake in deciding the mix between the private and public transport operations. Where the passengers' amenities and comforts increase, the passengers' preference for such operations may also increase. Consequently, it may pave the way for higher share for STUs or private operations. Hence there is an immediate need to know the opinion of the passengers as to their preference for a particular transport system, and the level of travel satisfaction. The result of such a survey would be of immense help to the policy-makers in government and other authorities in arriving at a proper transport policy. This research work is a modest attempt in this direction.

7. OBJECTIVES OF THE STUDY

The overall objective of the study is to evaluate the performance of Pattukottai Azhagiri Transport Corporation Ltd., a state owned transport corporation. Apart from the physical and financial performance, the study aims at comparing PATC operations with that of private bus operation with regard to passengers' bus usage and preference and the level of passengers' satisfaction in these sectors. The specific objectives of the study are:

1. To review the progress of the public sector passenger road transport system in India and Tamil Nadu.
2. To review the performance of Pattukottai Azhagiri Transport Corporation Ltd.
3. To make a study on the bus usage profile and

preference of the passenger respondents in the North Arcot Region of Tamil Nadu.

4. To measure the level of passenger satisfaction of the sample respondents with regard to the PATC and private bus operation and to ascertain the relationship between the personal factors of the respondents and their travel satisfaction.
5. To suggest measures to improve passengers' satisfaction.

8. OPERATIONAL DEFINITIONS

1. Passenger Satisfaction

Passenger satisfaction means the satisfaction derived by the individual passenger on various aspects of their travel in buses such as comforts, punctuality, regularity, safety, reliability, crew behaviour and social responsibility. Passenger satisfaction has been measured in this study through a scale developed for this purpose by name 'Passenger Satisfaction Scale'. The extent of satisfaction derived by the individual passengers has been measured separately for their travel in PATC buses and in private buses.

2. Bus Usage Profile

Passengers come across buses operated by different agencies such as PATC, other government corporations and private operators. When a choice is possible, i.e., many buses of these different agencies are plied at the same or nearly the same timings as per the approved schedule, passengers are likely to choose a particular bus for their travel according to the satisfaction they derive from their travel in various buses as explained above. In this study, passengers have been required to rank the bus in which they mostly travel. Based on the ranks awarded, their usage profile has been studied. The procedure is explained in the appropriate chapter.

3. Passenger Preference

The respondents have been asked to give their preference for buses for their travel between the buses operated by the

PATC and Private operators.

4. North Arcot Region

North Arcot Region includes, North Arcot Ambedkar District, Tiruvannamalai Sambuvarayar District, Western part of South Arcot District and Northern part of Chingleput District of Tamil Nadu. These are the operational areas covered by the PATC.

5. Performance

The performance of the study unit—PATC—a public sector passenger Road Transport Corporation has been studied with reference to Physical performance, Financial performance, Quality of service, Social responsibility and the extent of passenger satisfaction, usage and preference by the travelling public.

The first chapter delineates the introduction, review of literature, statement of the problem, objectives, scheme of chapters. The second chapter reviews the operational performance of the Public Sector Passenger Road Transport. The third chapter focuses on the performance of Pattukottai Azhagiri Transport Corporation Limited. The fourth chapter analyses the bus usage profile of the respondents and passengers' preference between PATC and private bus operation in the study region. The fifth chapter gives a comparative study of the passengers' satisfaction in PATC and in private bus operation and the relationship between personal factors and passengers' satisfaction. The sixth chapter sums up the findings of the study and also suggests steps to improve the passengers' satisfaction as well as to improve the efficiency of PATC.

Notes and References

1. Bagade, M.V., "A New Look at Performance Appraisal of STUs", *Journal of Transport Management (JTM)*, April 1986, Pune: Central Institute of Road Transport, p. 15.
2. Performance Statistics of STUs 1988-89 and 1989-90, Pune: CIRT, p. 2.
3. Review of State Public Enterprises in Tamil Nadu, 1989-90, Madras: State Bureau of Public Enterprises (Finance Department), Government of Tamil Nadu, p. 5.
4. Murthy, S.S., 'Criteria for Evaluation of STUs', *JTM*, April 1986, Pune:

CIRT, pp. 6-14.

5. Bagade, M.V., 'A New Look at Performance Appraisal of STUs', *JTM*, April 1986, Pune: CIRT, pp. 15-20.
6. Rao, Hanumantha Ch., 'Comparative study of certain Traffic Parameters in selected STUs', *JTM*, February 1990, Pune: CIRT, pp. 11-24.
7. Patankar, P.G., 'Quality in Road Passenger Transport', *JTM*, November 1986, Pune: CIRT, pp. 5-13.
8. Swaroop Behara Anand, 'Methodologies for Augmentation of Bus Service on existing routes in STUs', *JTM*, September 1991, Pune: CIRT, pp. 5-9.
9. Deshmukh, A.R., 'Creative Accounting: A New Social Benefit Approach to Read the Balance Sheets of STUs: A Case of MSRTC', *JTM*, September 1991, Pune: CIRT, pp. 11-15.
10. Padam Sudarsanam, "Nationalisation of Passenger Road Transport—Looking Back and Looking Forward", *JTM*, November 1990, Pune: CIRT, pp. 30-38.
11. Mahesh Chand, 'Current Issues in Public Road Transport Management', *Lok Udyog*, August 1980, pp. 41-48.
12. Devasahayam, M.G., 'State Transport-Making Undertakings Profitable', *Economic Times*, 2nd December 1983.
13. David Maunder, *et. al.*, 'Matching Supply and Demand in India's Public Transport', *JTM*, July 1988, Pune: CIRT, pp. 13-16.
14. Raghunathan, V., *et. al.*, 'Passenger Transport in India—A Customers' Perspective', *JTM*, Sept. 1991, Pune: CIRT, pp. 17-21.
15. Arora, S.K., 'Economics of Management in Road Transport Industry', 1987, New Delhi: Deep & Deep Publications.
16. Singh, Ratan Kumar, 'Road Transport and Economic Development', 1988, New Delhi: Deep & Deep Publications.
17. Subrahmanyam, P., "Organisational Set-up of Road Transport", 1987, New Delhi: B.R. Publishing Corporation.
18. Sharma, Santosh, 'Productivity in Road Transport: A Study in Innovative Management', 1985, New Delhi: ASRTUs.
19. Armstrong-Wright, Alan and Thiriz Sebastian, 'Bus Services—Reducing costs, Raising Standards', World Bank Technical Paper No. 68, 1987, Washington: The World Bank.
20. Ossewaarde, J.M., 'Public Transport—Future Perspectives', *JTM*, Feb. 1990, Pune: CIRT, pp. 25-27.
21. Raman, A.V., 'The Rationale of Nationalisation of Passenger Road Transport', *JTM*, Oct. 1990, Pune: CIRT, pp. 5-10.
22. Bagade, M.V., 'What Ails State Transport', *JTM*, Dec. 1990, Pune: CIRT, pp. 19-24.
23. Rao, Hanumantha Ch., 'Nationalised Passenger Road Transport in India—A Perspective', *JTM*, May 1990, Pune: CIRT, p. 15-18.
24. Raman, A.V., 'Road Transport: Case against Privatisation', *Financial Express*, 10th July 1989.
25. Vijayakumar, K.C., "Operating Cost of Public Sector Transport Undertaking in India", *Lok Udyog*, August 1979, pp. 29-32.

26. Kulshrestha, D.K., "Management of State Road Transports in India", 1989, New Delhi: Inter-India Publications.

27. Rao, Panduranga, D., 'Dimensions of Rural Transportation', 1989, New Delhi: Inter-India Publications.

28. Patankar, P.G., "Road Passenger Transport in India", 1985, Pune: CIRT.

29. Padam Sudarsanam, "Bus Transport in India—The Structure, Management and Performance of Road Transport Corporation", 1990, Delhi: Ajanta Publications, (India).

30. Parmar, 'GSRTC Performance: Remedy to Recover losses', *Economic Times*, 11th November 1988.

31. Sriramula, C.T., *et al.*, 'V and J Services: A New concept in urban Transit in Madras', Dhingra, S.I. & Orpe, S.G. (Ed.), Transport System Studies—Analysis and policy proceedings, The National Conference, 1989, New Delhi: Tata MacGraw Hill.

32. Rao, Rajeswar, 'Management Effectiveness in Transport Operations—A Case Study of Delhi Transport Corporation', *Lok Udyog*, July 1982, pp. 11-21.

33. Chandra, Rajesh, 'Financial Performance of Delhi Transport Corporation: A Social Accounting Approach', *Nagarlok*, Jan.-Mar. 1991, pp. 17-35.

34. Halder, Dilip Kumar, 'Public Undertaking in Motor Bus Transportation in the city of Calcutta: An Economic Analysis and Programming Solutions', (Unpublished Ph.D. Thesis), 1969, Pune: University of Pune.

35. Bagade, M.V., 'Management Information System for Passenger Bus Transport Industry (A Special study of Maharashtra State Road Transport Corporation)', (unpublished Ph.D. Thesis), 1980, Pune: University of Pune.

36. Dixit, M.C., 'A Study of the Pune Municipal Transport Administration with reference to its service efficiency from 1959 Onwards', (Unpublished Ph.D. Thesis), 1972, Pune: University of Pune.

37. Gandhi, Jegadish P., 'State Transport Undertakings in Southern States: A Comparative Study', *Southern Economist*, Oct. 1989, pp. 26-30.

38. Kulkarni, S.D., 'Working and Problems of Passenger Road Transport in Maharashtra', (Unpublished Ph.D. Thesis), 1978, Pune: University of Pune.

39. Diandas, J., 'Private Bus Transport in Sri Lanka—It's performance, productivity and manpower', 1988, Colombo: Fridrich-Ebert-Stiftung.

40. Pillai Thalavai, "Transport Corporations in Tamil Nadu—A Study of Performance of Pandiyan Roadways Corporation Ltd. and Cholan Roadways Corporation Ltd.", (Unpublished Ph.D. Thesis), 1991, Madurai: Madurai Kamaraj University.

41. Feibel Charles and Walters, A.A., 'Ownership and Efficiency in Urban Buses', World Bank Staff Working Paper No. 371, 1980, Washington, World Bank.

42. Carpetis, S., *et al.*, 'The Supply and Quality of Rural Transport Services in Developing Countries—A Comparative Review', World Bank Staff Working Paper No. 654, 1984, Washington: World Bank.

43. Walters, A.A., 'Cost and Scale of Bus Service', World Bank Staff Working

Paper No. 325, 1979, Washington: World Bank.

44. Hensher, David A., "Productive Efficiency and Ownership of Urban Bus Services", Transportation 14: 1987, pp. 209-25.
45. Downs Charles, "Private and Public Local Bus Services Compared: The Case of New York City", *Transportation Quarterly*, Vol. 42, No. 4, October 1988, pp. 553-70.
46. Umrigar, F.S., *et al.*, 'Exploring the scope of private participation for urban public transport supply in India', *Transport Reviews*, 1989, Vol. 9, No. 2, p. 135-46.
47. Dutta, P., 'Private Bus Options', *JTM*, Feb. 1991, Pune: CIRT, pp. 33-36.
48. Performance Statistics of STUs 1980-81 and 1989-90.
49. Upasani, S.P., 'Is Privatisation of Transport the answer to our problem?', *JTM*, June 1990, Pune: CIRT, pp. 13-15.

2

Operational Performance of Public Sector Passenger Road Transport

1. INTRODUCTION

In this chapter an attempt is made to review the current scenario of the operation of the Nationalised bus service. It has been divided into two parts, the first part dealing with operational performance of STUs in India and the second with that of the Tamil Nadu STUs.

2. ROAD TRANSPORT IN INDIA

Road Transport has come to occupy a pivotal position in the overall transport system of the country, which comprises several modes of transport, amongst which rail and road transport predominate. Especially for short and medium distance travel, bus sector dominates because of their flexibility and accessibility to a large number of villages and towns. Buses even compete with railways on certain long distance routes by offering night services. For instance, Bombay-Mangalore (about 500 km) on the West Coast is well served by buses. In some routes, such as Jaipur-Gwalior and Jaipur-Bhopal, buses have an edge over trains because one or more train changes are involved and the timings/connections are often inconvenient.[1] Moreover, bus services are more frequent and time-suited; it is easy to get a ticket at short notice and easier still to get a seat thereafter. All this has meant a steady shift of passenger traffic from rail to road as can be seen from Table 2.1

TABLE 2.1

Trends in Share of Road and Rail Passenger Movement

(Passenger Kilometres in percentage)

Year	*Road Share %*	*Rail Share %*
1951	37.8	62.2
1961	57.2	42.8
1971	69.0	31.0
1981	76.0	24.0
1985	80.2	19.8

Source: Singh, Mohinder and Kadiyali, L.R., "Crisis in Road Transport", 1990, Delhi: Konark Publishers Pvt. Ltd., p. 8.

It is noted that there has been a sharp shift in the share of the railway in the total traffic. The share of road transport has been increasing over the years, from 38 per cent in 1951 to 80 per cent in 1985, whereas the share of railways has come down from 62 per cent to 20 per cent during this period.

While comparing the future demand for buses and other modes of travel such as cars and jeeps, the demand for buses will be more than that for other modes. It is estimated by the Planning Group that the passenger traffic demand for buses will increase at the rate of 8 per cent whereas that for cars, taxis and jeeps will increase at the rate of 7 per cent compound per annum.[2] The projections based on these estimated rates are given in Table 2.2

TABLE 2.2

Estimates of Passenger Kilometers (Billion)

Years	*Mode of Transport*	
	Bus	*Car, Jeep, Taxi*
1985 (Base year)	751.49	47.35
1990	1104.19	66.41
1995	1622.41	93.14
2000	2383.85	130.64
Compound Rate of Growth	8%	7%

Source: Patankar, P.G., "Modern Trends in STUs", *Journal of Transport Management*, Oct. 1989, Pune: CIRT, p. 6.

3. EMERGENCE OF STATE TRANSPORT UNDERTAKINGS IN INDIA

Bus operations in India began mostly with single vehicle owners. Excessive competition and concentration on the more popular routes so as to maximise their profit was not unusual. Alarmed at the trend the government enacted the Motor Vehicles Act of 1939 which laid for the first time the basis for proper control and co-ordination of road transport service. It gave powers to state authorities to restrict the number of licences for buses on any route and to control their operations. By then expert opinion had suggested controlled monopoly as the only answer to the evils of unhindered and selfish competition among bus operators. It was again felt that speedy, regulai and comfortable bus services could best be offered by large companies and not by small scattered owners. Persuasion as well as compulsion was tried by several state governments to organize individual operators into bigger and economically viable units. Even attempts were made to bring the private sector in groups forming co-operative societies, which attempts however, were not successful due to the conflicting objectives of the parties concerned. Joint operations of government and private buses were also tried without success.

The national government that took office after

independence was of the opinion that the solution lay in nationalizing the bus industry. Various state governments amended the Motor Vehicles Act in 1947-48 to enable them to cancel stage carriage permits as a part of the policy of nationalization. The Road Transport Corporation Act was passed in 1950 empowering the State Governments to form public sector corporations to run bus services. Government involvement in bus operations became substantial. States like Maharashtra, Gujarat and Haryana operate completely nationalized bus services. The southern states have also gone for extensive public sector bus services. Andhra Pradesh has gone for total nationalization and the remaining states opted for partial nationalization.

The recently enacted Motor Vehicles Act, 1988 aims at promoting adequate bus transport service through liberal issue of permits to "any one making application anywhere, any time". Simultaneously, while powers of state transport undertakings for notifying schemes of nationalization of areas and routes as well rest with the state/regional transport authorities, preferential treatment of STUs in the grant of permits have been withdrawn. This has led to fear among STUs, who feel that the "opening up of the flood-gate of passenger road transport has been dealt a severe blow. It is a matter of concern that in the last ten years or so the share of passenger road transport in the hands of STUs, measured in terms of fleet strength has progressively declined from 48.9 per cent in 1977 to 35.6 per cent in 1990 and STUs in terms of fleet strength are practically back at the pre-1956 position.[3]

4. OPERATIONAL PERFORMANCE OF STUs IN INDIA

Operational performance of STUs is reflected in few indexes which are discussed below:

1. Fleet Strength, Passengers Carried and Kilometres Operate

There are 67 STUs, of which 21 are Corporations, 27 are Companies, 8 are Government Departments and 11 are Municipal Undertakings. Fifty-nine of them own 99.8 per cent of total passenger fleet of STUs as on March 1989. The combined fleet strength of STUs as on 31.03.89 was 99,219 passenger buses.

They operated nearly 375 billion passenger kms in the year 1988-89 or 36 per cent of the total passenger movement by road. They carried 985.5 crores of passengers in 1976-77. The number of passengers has increased to 2011.15 crores in 1988-89, recording an annual growth rate of 6.12. Next to Indian Railways, STUs account for the highest number of persons employed viz. 7.22 lakh.[4] It is estimated that by the turn of the century, passenger road transport would account for 2384 billion Passengers kms per annum (Table 2.2). The growth of STUs in the number of passenger buses and effective kms. operated during the last decade has been indicated in Table 2.3 from which it is observed that number of buses have gone up to 99.22 thousands in 1988-89 from 69.55 thousands in 1988-89, accounting for 42 per cent increase. Similarly, the effective kms operated by all these buses have also increased from 533.56 crore to 879 kms during the same period.

TABLE 2.3

Fleet Strength and Effective Kilometers Run by STUs (1980-81 to 1988-89)

Year	*No. of Buses*	*Effective kms (in crore)*
1980-81	69550	533.56
1981-82	73890	569.78
1982-83	75708	584.51
1983-84	76639	618.82
1984-85	80184	637.63
1985-86	83986	675.66
1986-87	88809	761.49
1987-88	94823	821.74
1988-89	99219	879.00

Source: Improvement in STUs, 1990, Pune: CIRT, p. 3.

2. Fleet Utilization

The percentage of fleet utilization to fleet held has been in the increasing order. It has gone up from 84 per cent in 1981-82 to 88 per cent in 1988-89, showing an increase by 4 per cent (Table 2.4). It is also noted that the increase has been consistent

EXHIBIT 1

Fleet Strength of STUs in India

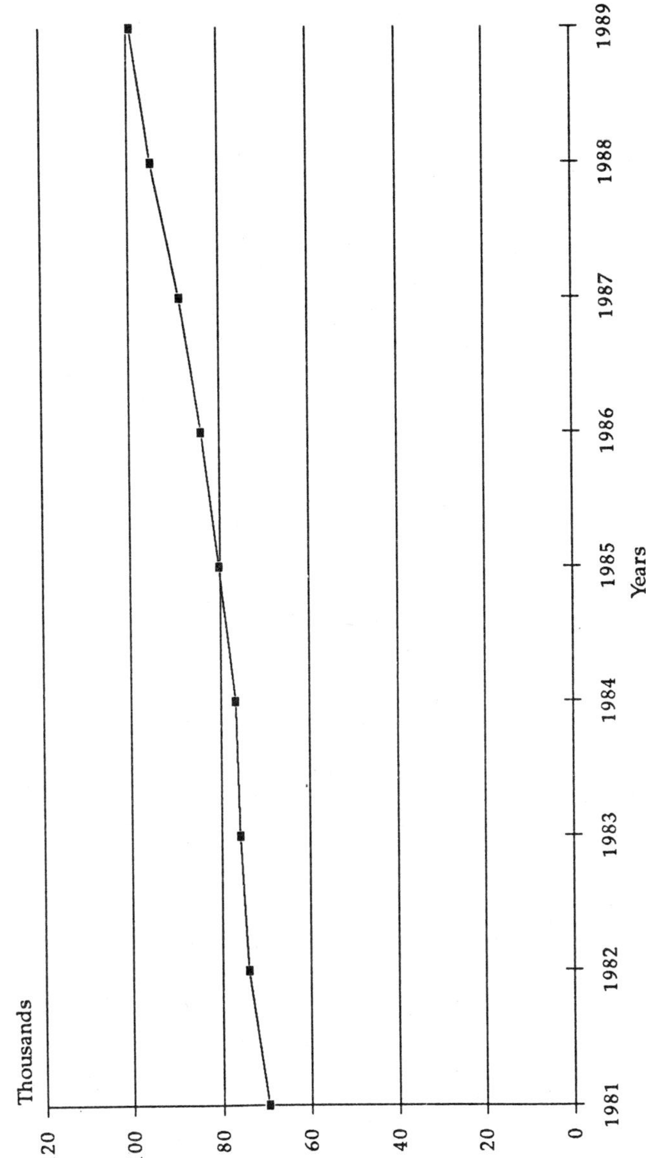

TABLE 2.4

Operational Performance of STUs in India
(1981-82 to 1988-89)

Item/Year	*1981-82*	*1982-83*	*1983-84*	*1984-85*	*1985-86*	*1986-87*	*1987-88*	*1988-89*
Fleet Utilization (%)	84	82	84	84	85	88	87	88
Capital Productivity (in kms per fleet per day)	219.4	212.7	221.1	219.6	227.0	238.9	244.4	253.7
Man-Power Productivity (bus kms per employee per day)	27.4	26.9	28.4	28.1	28.7	30.2	31.7	33.22
Kms per litre of diesel (KMPL)	4.10	4.02	4.07	4.07	4.13	4.21	4.24	4.25
Bus-Staff Ratio (Buses on road)	9.65	9.78	9.76	9.75	9.50	9.02	8.86	8.63
Break-Downs per 10,000 Eff. kms	1.29	1.03	1.02	0.93	0.94	0.75	0.71	0.65
Accident per lakh kms	0.81	0.82	0.80	0.73	0.65	0.63	0.58	0.57

Source: Performance Statistics of STUs 1980-81 to 1988-89, Pune: CIRT.

over the period except in the year 1982-83 when it declined to 82 per cent from 84 per cent in the previous year and in 1987-88 when there was a marginal decline.

3. Capital Productivity

The kms operated per bus has also been in the upward trend. From 219.4 kms, it has gone up to a level of 253 kms recording an increase of 34 kms between 1981-82 and 1988-89.

4. Man-Power Productivity

The average kilometres operated by an employee per day has been impressive. From 27.4 kms in 1981-82, it went up to 33.22 kms recording an increase of 5.82 kms during the period, which is 21 per cent. The bus-staff ratio has been in the decreasing order, which shows better performance. The bus-staff ratio has been reduced to 8.63 per bus in 1988-89 from 9.65 per bus in 1981-82.

5. Fuel Conservation

Kilometres operated per litre of diesel has increased through the concerted efforts of the STUs. From 4.10 in 1981-82 it has consistently increased and reached a level of 4.25 kms in 1988-89.

6. Break-down and Accidents

In the sphere of quality of service also, the STUs have fared well, which is indicated by less number of break-downs and accidents. The data pertaining to these factors have been in the decreasing order, the former has come down from 1.29 per 10,000 effective kms. in 1981-82 to 0.65 in 1988-89 and the accident per one lakh kilometres has come down to 0.81 in 1988-89 from 0.57 in 1981-82.

7. Financial Performance

Table 2.5 exhibits the losses incurred by the STUs during the period 1980-81 to 1988-89. It is noted from the table that during all these years the STUs have incurred losses though the amount of loss fluctuates over the period and ranges from Rs. 215.81 crores (1980-81) to Rs. 510.96 crores (1986-87). The cumulative losses of STUs have increased from Rs. 215.81 crores in 1981-82 to Rs. 3175.06 crores.

TABLE 2.5

Extent of Losses of STUs (1980-81 to 1988-89)

(Rs. in crores)

Year	*Loss*	*Cumulative Loss*
1980-81	215.81	215.81
1981-82	309.16	524.97
1982-83	237.90	762.87
1983-84	297.41	1060.28
1984-85	415.10	1475.38
1985-86	462.15	1937.53
1986-87	510.96	2448.49
1987-88	298.29	2746.78
1988-89	428.28	3175.06

Source: Performance Statistics of STUs, 1980-81 to 1989-90, CIRT, Pune.

It may be noted that Operating Ratio has been less than 100 per cent (it ranges between 92 and 98.2 per cent)[5] in each year denoting that the cost of service is met from the revenue from it. Inspite of the inspiring performance of STUs, in terms of the operating ratio, the financial performance on the basis of total expenditure and revenue is not healthy as revealed in Table 2.5. The causes for the continued financial losses seem to be external such as high incidence of tax, operating uneconomic services and unremunerative fare. In this regard, it is pertinent to mention here the observations made by the Planning Commission, "Financial viability of SRTUs has been seriously impaired by inflexible fares, an environment of rising costs, concessional travel, uneconomic routes and above all high level of taxation. Periodic increases in prices of key inputs have pushed up the cost of vehicle manufactures, the burden of which has been passed on to the undertakings. The position has come to such that unless these undertakings are supported with lower taxes and given the flexibility to adjust fares to match their costs, they may become a serious burden on the economy."[6]

5. NATIONALISED BUS SERVICE IN TAMIL NADU

1. Profile of Tamil Nadu

Tamil Nadu accounting for 7.5 per cent of India's population and 4.3 per cent of geographical area has the longest surfaced road length (78.1 per cent) in the country. The length of roads has increased more than four-fold since 1961, from 38.192 kms to 1,31,516 kms as on 31st March 1984 and now Tamil Nadu occupies third rank next to Maharashtra and Uttar Pradesh in length of roads. More than 55 per cent of villages are connected by all-weather roads. The road intensity per 100 square km in Tamil Nadu (71.7 kms) is higher than the all India rate of 65.3 kms. However, the density of road kms per lakh of population in the state is only 227 as against the All-India density of 391.7 kms. Maharashtra had the largest number of motor vehicles followed by Tamil Nadu which had 2.21 lakh motor vehicles on road in 1977 and 9.58 lakh in 1987.[7]

2. Phases of Bus Nationalisation

1. Period of Evolution (1947-67)

The Tamil Nadu Government's decision to nationalise the motor transport service was launched in Madras City in October 1947. Stage by stage, by July 1948 the entire service in Madras City was nationalised. During 1956, after the States re-organisation, services already nationalised in Kanyakumari district came under the State Transport Department. The first long distance express service was started in August 1959 based on the policy that all routes exceeding 120 miles should be exclusively operated by the Department with express services and several long distance routes were opened from time to time.

2. Period of Exploration (1967-72)

With a view to extending nationalisation of bus transport by stages, the Government decided in June 1967, that the following types of bus routes should be nationalized as and when the permits of the private operator expired:

(i) all routes of 75 miles and above, both ordinary and express services;

(ii) all routes radiating from or terminating in Madras City irrespective of length; and

(iii) all routes in Kanyakumari district which are radiating from or terminating in that district.

The Government also decided that future development of the above said routes should be undertaken exclusively by the Department.

The Government considered it necessary to set up a public limited company to take over and operate the services in the greater Madras and Chinglepet District, leaving the mofussil services, long distance routes and Kanyakumari Branch to be operated by the Department. Accordingly, a public limited company be name Pallavan Transport Corporation Limited was established and it took over the transportation system in Madras and Chinglepet district with effect from 1st January 1972.

Simultaneously, the Government declared the need to nationalise the commanding heights of the economy in order to promote a socialistic order. Accordingly, the Government passed the Tamil Nadu Fleet Operations and Stage Carriages (Acquisition) Act, 1971 with the objective of nationalising all passenger transport divisions of transport undertakings having 50 or more bus permits. Under the provisions of the Act, the buses from the erstwhile private companies such as Southern Roadways Private Limited, the Raman and Raman Private Limited, the Sri Rama Vilas Services Limited and ABT Limited were acquired. Three Government owned Public Limited Companies were founded in 1972, for the purpose of taking over and operating the nationalised services. Pandian Roadways Corporation was incorporated with an authorised capital of Rs. 5.25 crores for the management of the bus transport system in Madurai and Ramanathapuram Districts. The Cholan Roadways Corporation was set up with an authorised Capital of Rs. 3 crores for running the passenger transport system in the districts of Thanjavur, South Arcot and Tiruchirapalli. The Cheran Transport Corporation with an authorised capital of Rs. 1 crore was established for maintaining road transport services in the districts of Coimbatore and Nilgiris.

3. Period of Expansion (1972-89)

As the nationalisation process gathered momentum and the fleet strength rose, the Government felt that it was desirable and necessary to create more Corporations at the rate of one for each district except for the smaller ones like Niligiris, Pudukkotti and Kanyakumari. Each Corporation may have a fleet strength ranging from 350 to 600 buses. The five-member committee headed by C.R. Pattabi Raman which was set up by the Tamil Nadu Government in 1976 to go into the structure and performance of road transport corporations and the ancillary Engineering Corporations, had made as many as 236 recommendations encompassing the entire gamut of transport operations. Based on the recommendations of the Pattabi Raman Committee Report, a decision was taken to bifurcate the Corporations having more than 600 buses with area of operation being co-terminus broadly with the Revenue District.

With progressive nationalisation, bifurcation of the bigger units and the establishment of new Corporations, the number of Transport Corporations increased to 16 in Tamil Nadu (Table 2.6). During the 1970's Seven Corporations were found and in 80's another eight were added. The PTC was trifurcated into Thiruvalluvar Transport Corporation (exclusively for long distance Express Service) PTC (District) and PTC (Metro).

In 1970 out of 7,792 passenger vehicles in Tamil Nadu, the State Corporations accounted for 1975 which was 25 per cent and in 1980 the share of STUs in the total number of stage carriages increased to 55 per cent (6,243 buses). Further this share has gone up and reached a level of 13,299 buses (70 per cent) against the total of 18,937 buses leaving only 5,638 buses (30 per cent) in the private sector (Table 2.7).

3. Centre-wise Break-up of Public and Private Buses in Tamil Nadu

The data pertaining to operations of buses by private and STUs are shown in Table 2.8, from which it is observed that STUs operate all Metro services and their share in Madras City in 95 per cent and the rest 5 per cent is covered by other Mofussil

TABLE 2.6

State Transport Corporations in Tamil Nadu

Sl. No.	*Name of the Corporation*	*Date of Commencement of Business*	*Principal areas of operation*	*Fleet Strength as on 31.3.89*
1	2	3	4	5
1.	Pallavan Transport Corporation Ltd. (PTC)	01.01.72	Madras Metro	2202
2.	Cheran Transport Corporation Ltd. (CTC)	01.03.72	Coimbatore and Nilgiris Dts	1259
3.	Cholan Roadways Corporation Ltd. (CRC)	01.03.72	Thanjavur and Tiruchi Dts	703
4.	Pandian Roadways Corporation Ltd. (PRC)	17.01.72	Madurai Kamarajar Dt	865
5.	Anna Transport Corporation Ltd. (ATC)	15.02.73	Salem Dt	694
6.	Kattabomman Transport Corporation Ltd. (KTC)	01.01.74	Tirunelveli Kattabomman and Chidambarannar Dts	727
7.	Thanthai Periyar Tpt Corporation Ltd. (TPTC)	16.01.75	South Arcot and Southern areas of Chenglepet Dts	904
8.	Thiruvalluvar Transport Corporation Ltd. (TTC)	01.04.80	Entire State of Tamil Nadu Express Service	829
9.	Pattukottai Azhagiri Tpt Corporatoin Ltd. (PATC)	01.12.82	North Arcot and Northern areas of Chenglepet Dts	882
10.	Nesamony Transport Corporation Ltd. (NTC)	01.04.83	Kanyakumari District Podukottai	540
11.	Marudhu Pandiyar Tpt Corporation Ltd. (MPTC)	01.04.83	Ramnad and Pasumpon Dts	659
12.	Jeeva Transport Corporation Ltd. (JTC)	01.04.83	Periyar Dt	670

(Contd.)

1	2	3	4	5
13.	Dheeran Cinnamalai Tpt Corporation Ltd. (DCTC)	01.04.84	Tiruchirapalli Dt	634
14.	Rani Mangammal Transport Corporation Ltd. (RMTC)	01.04.86	Anna Dist.	574
15.	Annai Satya Transport Corporation Ltd. (ASTC)	01.04.87	Dharmapuri Dt	449
16.	M.G.R. Transport Corporation Ltd. (MGRTC)	01.04.92	Chengai M.G.R. Dt.	636*

* As on 01.04.92.

Source: Review of State Public Sector Enterprises in Tamil Nadu, 1989-90, State Bureau of Public Enterprises (Finance Department), Madras.

TABLE 2.7

Total Number of Buses in Public and Private Sectors in Tamil Nadu

Year	*No. of Buses*		*Total*
	Public	*Private*	
1965	1076 (17)	5141 (83)	6217
1970	1975 (25)	5817 (75)	7792
1975	4252 (47)	4848 (53)	9100
1980	6243 (55)	5064 (45)	11307
1981	6769 (57)	5083 (43)	11852
1982	7551 (60)	5043 (40)	12594
1983	8058 (61)	5081 (39)	13139
1984	8286 (62)	5072 (38)	13358
1985	8869 (63)	5161 (37)	14030
1986	9671 (64)	5279 (35)	14950
1987	10863 (67)	5446 (33)	16309
1988	11616 (68)	5487 (32)	17103
1989	12640 (69)	5812 (31)	18452
1990	13299 (70)	5638 (30)	18937

Note: The figures within parentheses are percentages to the Row Totals.

Source: Records of Transport Department, Government of Tamil Nadu, Ezhilagam, Madras.

TABLE 2.8

Centre-wise Break-up of Public and Private Stage Carrier in Tamil Nadu (1989-90)

District/Centre	*Private*	*Public*	*Total*
Chinglepet	196 (37)	329 (63)	525
North Arcot	402 (40)	593 (60)	995
Thiruvannamalai	236 (40)	357 (60)	593
South Arcot	454 (47)	521 (53)	975
Salem	352 (46)	419 (54)	771
Namakkal	260 (43)	339 (57)	599
Dharmapuri	325 (45)	396 (55)	721
Trichi	407 (32)	854 (68)	1261
Thanjavur	202 (28)	511 (72)	713
Pudukottai	138 (35)	258 (65)	396
Nagappattinam	142 (36)	254 (64)	396
Karur	145 (41)	210 (59)	355
Ramnad	60 (22)	215 (78)	275
Virudhunagar	185 (38)	300 (62)	485
Sivagangai	126 (30)	293 (70)	419
Madurai	266 (24)	852 (76)	1118
Dindugal	292 (37)	505 (63)	797
Thirunelveli	241 (28)	626 (72)	867
Tutucorin	153 (42)	207 (58)	360
Coimbatore	284 (29)	681 (71)	965
Pollachi	228 (36)	406 (64)	634
Erode	362 (51)	349 (49)	711
Madras	182 (05)	3824 (95)	4006
Total	5638	13299	18937

Source: Records of Transport Department, Madras: Government of Tamil Nadu.

buses. The other districts in which STUs have larger share are Ramnad (78 per cent) and Madurai (76 per cent). The centres where STUs' share is relatively less are Erode (49 per cent) followed by South Arcot (53 per cent), Salem (54 per cent), Dharmapuri (54 per cent), Namakkal (57 per cent) and Tuticorin (58 per cent). In the rest of the centres the STUs' share ranges between 60 and 65 per cent.

4. Service Mix of Public and Private Buses in Tamil Nadu

The service mix, i.e., operation of different types of services, such as Metropolitan, City/Town, Mofussil ordinary and Mofussil express services are shown in Table 2.9. Mofussil ordinary services account for 49 per cent in 1989-90 followed by City/Town service, Metro service and Mofussil express service. In comparison of the present services with that in 1979-80, Metro and Mofussil express services almost remain the same while Mofussil ordinary services have declined by 11 per cent and City/Town services have increased by 13 per cent. With regard to the share of public and private sectors in the different category of services, it is observed that in the case of Metro services almost 100% are with the STUs, and in the case of City/Town and mofussil express services the STUs have about 80 per cent share in the total fleets. Whereas in the case of the mofussil ordinary services it has share of 57 per cent in 1989-90.

The DMK Government, which speeded up the process of bus nationalisation in Tamil Nadu during 1970s, announced that complete nationalisation of passenger transport system was the ultimate objective of future transport policy. The present AIADMK Government also aims at total nationalisation. On 01.04.1992 a new Transport Corporation has been set up at Kancheepuram by bifurcating the PATC and naming it after the former Chief Minister M.G. Ramachandran, with a fleet strength of 636, having the entire Chengai M.G.R. district as its operational area.

The existing Transport Corporations together were operating a fleet of 13,543 buses carrying every day nearly 4 lakh passengers and employing 82,000 persons. Out of the total investment of Rs. 1671.02 crores made by Tamil Nadu Government in all the statutory Corporations covering various industries and services till the year 1989-90, the passenger transport sector alone accounted for Rs. 223.12 lakhs (nearly 14 per cent).[8] The Government expects the transport corporations to function in accordance with sound commercial principles as far as practicable, consistent with their responsibility as public utility concerns, dealing with a vital sector of importance to the community as a whole.

TABLE 2.9

Service Mix of Transport Operations in Tamil Nadu (1979-80 and 1989-90)

	Type of Service	*1979-80*			*1989-90*		
		Public Sector	*Private Sector*	*Total*	*Public Sector*	*Private Sector*	*Total*
1.	Metropolitan Service	1583	6	1589	2185	6	2191
		(100)	(-)		(100)	(-)	
2.	City/Town Service	1378	1058	2436	5098	1212	6310
		(57)	(43)		(81)	(19)	(37)
3.	Mofussil Ordinary Service	2470	3484	5951	4635	3561	8196
		(41)	(59)		(57)	(43)	
4.	Mofussil Express Service	313	25	338	101	31	132
		(93)	(7)		(77)	(23)	
	Total	5744	4573	10317	12019	4810	16829

Source: Administrative Reports (1979-80 and 1989-90) of Transport Department, Madras: Government of Tamil Nadu.

6. PERFORMANCE REVIEW OF STUs IN TAMIL NADU

The performance of Tamil Nadu STUs has been dealt with in the following pages. It is discussed under the following headings: (i) Physical Performance, (ii) Financial Performance, (iii) Quality of Service, and (iv) Social Benefits.

1. Physical Performance

It is significant to note that the physical performance of TNSTCs has shown an increasing trend right from their inception. Table 2.10 shows the progress made by TNSTCs from the year 1976-77 to 1988-89. It is noted that the fleet strength has increased from 4,853 in 1976-77 to 12,695 in 1988-89 there by indicating a rise of over 156 per cent over the period of 13 years. Pallavan Corporation tops the list with a fleet strength of 2202 in 1989-90 followed by CTC with 1259 buses and TPTC with 904 buses. The minimum number of buses (449) is with the ASTC. During the above period the maximum number of replacement of buses took place during the last 4 years, i.e. from 1985-86 to 1988-89, when 1620, 1270, 1619 and 1281 buses respectively were replaced. It is also noted that the maximum augmentation took place in the year 1986-87 when 1013 buses were added to the service. In the year 1987-88 and 1988-89, 530 and 539 buses were augmented. Similarly the number of routes served by TNSTCs has also increased significantly, from 2045 in 1976-77 to 7028 routes in 1988-89 recording an increase of more than three times. The maximum addition to the existing routes took place in the year 1986-87 in which 943 routes were added. It is pertinent to mention here that during the same year the maximum number of buses were added (1030). Passengers carried per day also increased by three times, from 37.77 lakhs in 1976-77 to 119.8 lakhs in 1988-89.

It is also noted that the percentage of fleets operated to fleets held (Fleet Utilisation) by the TNSTCs has steadily increased from 87.4 per cent in 1976-77 to 92.6 per cent in 1988-89, reflecting high rate of fleet utilization in Tamil Nadu and also it is well above the all India STUs level of 88 per cent in 1988-89.[9] The ratio between operated km to scheduled km (km efficiency percentage) has shown an increasing trend from 93.9 per cent in 1976-77 to 97.9 per cent in 1988-89, showing an increase by 4 per cent. The increasing trend is also reflected in high fuel efficiency

TABLE 2.10

Physical and Operational Performance of STUs in Tamil Nadu

Year	*Fleet Strength*	*Fleet Utilisation %*	*Effective Kms run (in lakhs)*	*Km Efficiency*	*No. of Routes*	*Avr. No. of passengers carried per day (in lakhs)*	*KMPL*	*Occupancy Ratio*	*VMR**
1976-77	4953	87.4	4.490	93.9	2045	37.77	NA	70.4	7.4
1977-78	5068	87.4	4644	94.0	2177	40.93	NA	74.1	7.4
1978-79	5601	89.6	5192	94.8	2567	48.81	3.77	80.6	7.3
1979-80	6389	89.8	6051	94.4	3061	57.95	3.74	80.5	7.5
1980-81	7082	90.9	7004	95.3	3496	64.82	3.76	79.2	7.6
1981-82	7909	90.8	8097	96.2	3962	66.25	3.82	69.5	7.5
1982-83	8408	91.5	8666	96.9	4253	72.93	3.80	72.1	7.4
1983-84	8466	91.7	9925	97.6	4358	77.02	3.86	72.6	7.4
1984-85	9242	92.8	9578	97.6	4706	87.00	3.93	75.9	7.2
1985-86	10271	92.6	11098	97.8	5553	93.82	3.97	73.2	7.4
1986-87	11368	92.5	12720	98.0	6410	103.55	4.05	71.8	7.3
1987-88	12066	92.9	14029	97.8	6747	108.11	4.06	68.5	7.3
1988-89	12695	92.6	15335	97.9	7028	119.80	4.05	70.5	7.3

* VMR=Vehicle-Man Ratio.

Source: The Performance of Tamil Nadu STUs from 1976-77 to 1988-89, Madras: Chairman Cell, Transport Department, Government of Tamil Nadu.

EXHIBIT 2

Fleet Strength of STUs in Tamil Nadu

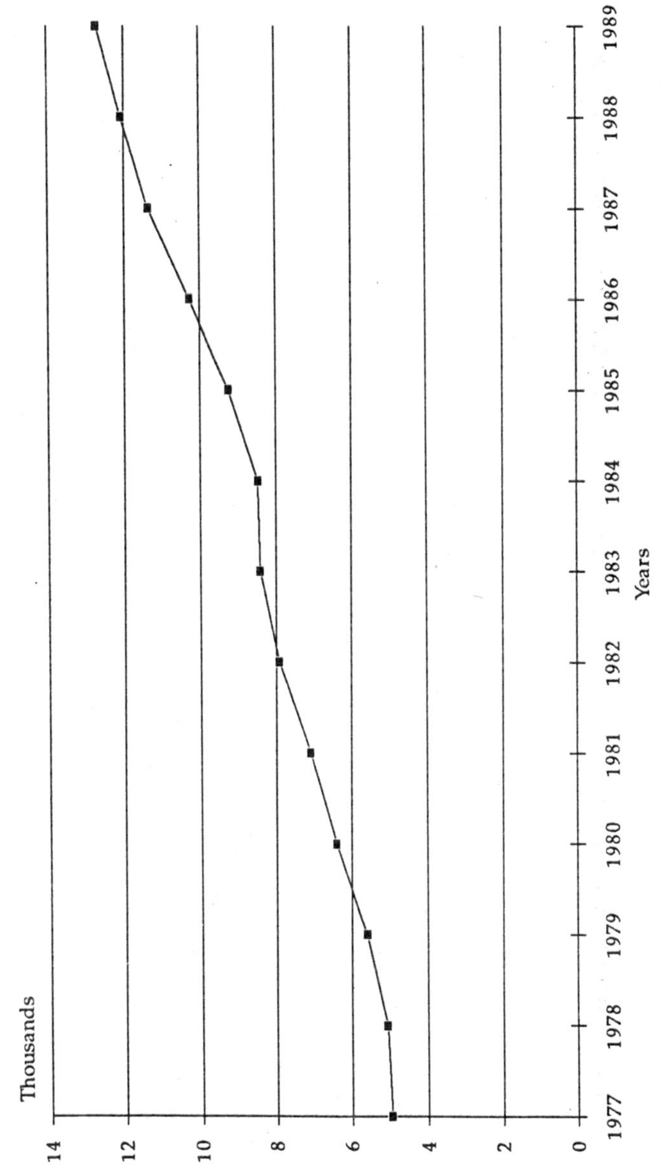

EXHIBIT 3

No. of Passengers Carried Per Day by Tamil Nadu State Transport Corporations' Buses

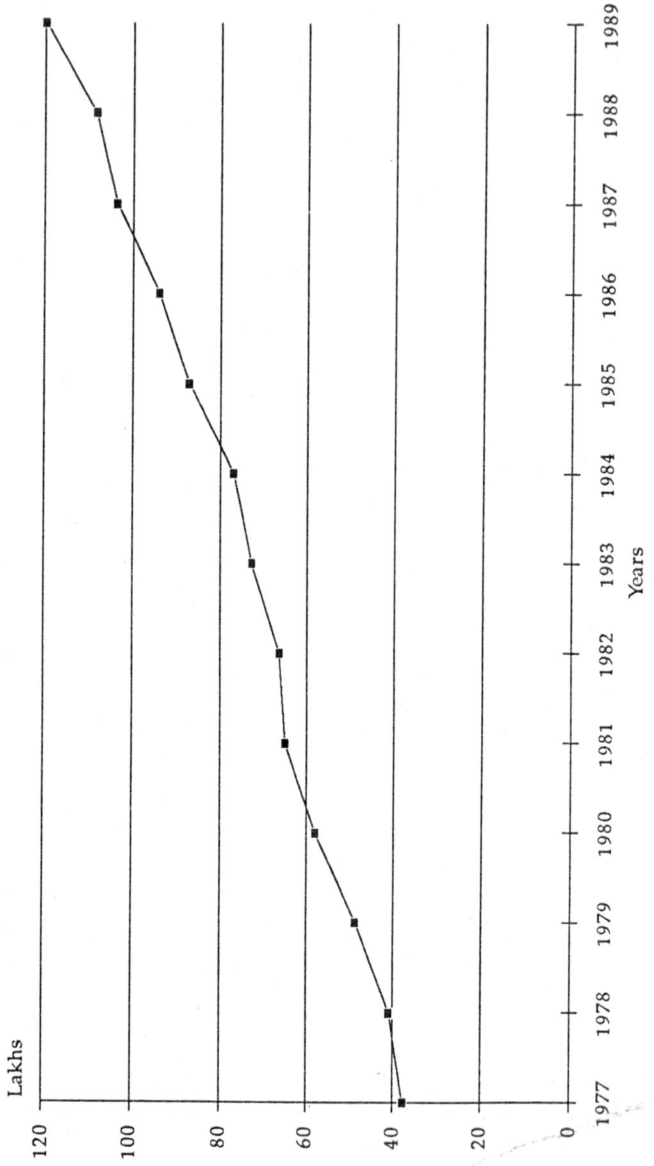

Lakhs

120
100
80
60
40
20
0

1977 1978 1979 1980 1981 1982 1983 1984 1985 1986 1987 1988 1989

Years

of TNSTCs. It speeded up from 3.6 km per litre of diesel in 1976-77 to 3.96 km in 1988-89, in the case of city/town service, it is also to be noted that in the year 1987-88 it has touched an all time high of 4 km and in the case of mofussil services it has increased from 3.87 to 4.17 km during the same period, the overall KMPL for both city/town and mofussil services has increased from 3.77 km in 1978-79 to 4.05 km in 1988-89.

The occupancy ratio (OR) of all STC's in Tamil Nadu ranges between 68.5 per cent (1987-88) and 80.6 per cent (1978-79) during the study period. In the case of JTC and DCTC the OR ranges low between 60.2 and 67.9 per cent, it ranges high between 79.2 and 89.8 per cent in the case of Pallavan during the years 1976-77 and 1988-89. The comparatively low OR can be attributed to running uneconomic routes/trips under social obligations by the STCs.

Number of persons engaged to operate a bus (Vehicle-Man Ratio) is another indicator reflecting the efficiency of the undertaking. A declining Vehicle-Man Ratio (VMR) is indicative of better performance. The data in Table 2.9 reveal that VMR in TNSTCs has increased from 7.4 in 1976-77 to 7.6 in 1980-81. It is observed that it has declined from 1981-82 onwards and touched the ratio of 7.3 in 1988-89. This is very much low against the norm prescribed by All India Association of Road Transport Undertaking at 9.0. It is also noted that while high VMR is found in the case of TTC where it ranges from 10.5 to 8.9 and a low ratio in the case of TPTC ranging between 7.0 and 6.6.

A significant aspect of public bus service is its penetration into hitherto inaccessible rural areas. The total number of villages benefited were 152 in 1976-77 which increased to 323 in 1988-89, thereby brining 9,418 villages into the network of bus transport service. In 1976-77, the bus service benefited 1.85 lakhs people in the above villages. The number of villages benefited increased to 3.14 lakhs in 1988-89, thereby covering an aggregate of 130.59 lakh people in those villages. It is to be noted that now the State Government is committed to press bus services into villages with a population of 1000 or more before the end of the year 1992.[10]

On 28th March 1990 the Government announced that students studying upto VIII standard would be given free bus passes for travel from their residence to school. This was implemented. The STCs also extend free travel concession to blind persons/physically handicapped persons, cancer patients and press correspondents and allow concessional fares to students in classes above VIIIth Standard. The transport corporations run buses in uneconomic routes also, to benefit the poorer sections of the society. In this regard, PTC tops the list, with 364 uneconomic routes out of 439 as at the end of 31st March 1990.[11]

2. Financial Performance

Transport is quite different from manufacturing and trading, especially in the hands of government. Its principal aim is to provide adequate service to the public rather than earning profits. Surplus/deficit over the total cost of operation, ratio of operating cost to operating revenue are the key parameters of financial performance of public Transport Corporations.

1. Revenue Trends

The gross revenue of all STCs in Tamil Nadu was Rs. 8464.44 lakhs in 1976-77, which went upto Rs. 66874.11 lakhs in 1988-89 recording an increase of about 7.9 times over the period of 13 years (Table 2.11). During the same period the cost also increased from Rs. 8421.3 lakhs in 1976-77 to Rs. 68152.99 lakhs in 1988-89 recording an increase of 8.1 times, which is marginally more than the increase in the gross revenue. This additional increase in the cost over the gross revenue has led the Transport Corporations to incur losses in the recent years. It has been noted from the table that during the years 1976-77 to 1979-80, all the Corporations put together had made profit, the highest being Rs. 443.83 lakhs in 1977-78, though certain individual Corporations incurred losses such as TPTC (Rs. 120.86 lakhs), followed by PATC (Rs. 18.57 lakhs). From the year 1980 onwards, the aggregate cost in all Transport Corporations exceeded the gross revenue and resulted in huge losses, especially during the year 1980-81 (Rs. 1318.3 lakhs) and in 1981-82 (Rs. 1791.54 lakhs) and from the year 1982-83 onwards the losses have been in the decreasing order and it is noted that in 1985-86 they earned a profit of Rs. 143.65 lakhs. From the very next year, i.e. 1986-87 they started incurring losses, Rs. 851.02 lakhs in 1986-87,

TABLE 2.11

Profit/Loss of State Transport Corporations of Tamil Nadu (1976-77 to 1988-89)

(Rs. in lakhs)

Year	*Revenue*	*Cost*	*Profit/ Loss*	*Cumulative Profit/ Loss*
1976-77	8464.44	8421.30	43.14	—
1977-78	9939.67	9495.82	443.85	486.99
1978-79	12224.39	12135.68	88.71	575.70
1979-80	15362.36	15265.56	96.80	672.50
1980-81	18235.03	19553.33	-1318.30	-645.80
1981-82	24427.11	26218.65	-1791.54	-2437.34
1982-83	28453.51	29142.46	-688.95	-3126.29
1983-84	30756.30	31041.42	-285.12	-3411.41
1984-85	33971.67	34205.66	-233.99	-3645.40
1985-86	44280.58	44136.93	143.65	-3501.75
1986-87	50272.89	51123.91	-851.02	-4352.77
1987-88	59059.55	61522.94	-2463.39	-6816.16
1988-89	66874.11	68152.99	-1278.88	-8095.04

Source: The Performance of Tamil Nadu State Transport Undertakings from 1976-77 to 1988-89, Madras: Chairman Cell, Transport Department, Government of Tamil Nadu.

Rs. 2463.99 lakhs in 1987-88 and Rs. 1278.88 lakhs in 1988-89. The cumulative profit/loss has been shown in Col. (iv). During the years 1976-77 to 1979-80 the aggregate profit stood at Rs. 672.5 lakhs and from the year 1980-81 to 1988-89 the cumulative loss of all TNSTCs has increased from Rs. 645.8 lakhs to Rs. 8095.04 lakhs recording an increase of over 12 times.

2. Earnings per Kilometre

The disquieting trends as further substantiated while analysing Transport Corporation's average Revenue/Cost per km operated. It is noted that from the year 1976-77 to 1979-80 and in the year 1984-85 (5 years) all the Corporations put together made profit per kilometre run on an average. The highest was 9.8 paise in the year 1977-78 followed by 7.4 paise in the year

EXHIBIT 4

Revenue and Cost of STUs in Tamil Nadu

1985-86 and during the other years the Corporations incurred losses. The maximum loss was in the year 1981-82 followed by 1986-87 and 1980-81.[12]

The individual Corporation-wise average cost has been given for the last three years of the study period, i.e. from 1986-87. It is noted from Table 2.12, that in the year 1986-87 five Corporations made surplus with PATC topping the list with 7.3 paise, closely followed by TPTC (7 paise), CTC (2 paise) and RMTC and CRC (1 paisa each). Among the remaining Corporations, the maximum loss was incurred by PTC (38.8 paise) followed by PRC (27 paise). In the year 1987-88, no Corporation made surplus. However, it has been noted that TPTC made no profit and no gain as its EPKM (421 paise) is equal to CPKM. The maximum loss was suffered by MPTC and CRC with a loss of 32 paise each, followed by PRC (27 paise) and KTC (26 paise). In the year 1988-89 only two Corporations viz., RMTC and ASTC made a marginal profit (1 paisa each) and two Corporations PATC and TPTC had break-even cost and rest of the corporations made loss, MPTC (22 paise), TTC (18 paise), PTC (17 paise) and PRC and KTC (15 paise each).

3. *Quality of Service*

Apart from physical and financial dimensions, quality of service is another area of vital importance for evaluation. Quality of service consists of punctuality, less number of break-downs and more safety.

The punctuality in departure as well as arrival timings of buses of TNSTCs was very satisfactory as these rates are close to 100 per cent except in the case of PTC which was 83.9 per cent in 1987-88 for both departure and arrival and it was 82.9 per cent for the year 1988-89.[13] Break-downs per 10,000 kms considerably declined, from 1.48 in 1976-77, to 0.32 in 1988-89, which is well below the all-India mark of 0.65 for the year 1988-89.[14] It is noted that the PTC has significantly brought down the number of break-downs, from 3.06 in 1976-77 to 0.80 per 10,000 kms recording a decrease of 26 per cent.

The number of accidents per lakh kms was 0.97 in 1976-77 which has increased to 1.0 in the year 1977-78 and almost remained the same for the subsequent 4 years and in the last 3

TABLE 2.12

Financial Results of TNSTCs (1986-87 to 1988-89)

(in paise)

	Tr. Under-takings	1986-87			1987-88			1988-89		
		EPKM	CPKM	Profit/ Loss Pkm	EPKM	CPKM	Profit/ Loss Pkm	EPKM	CPKM	Profit/ Loss Pkm
1.	PTC	493.4	532.2	-38.8	557.0	574.0	-17.0	561.0	578.0	-17
2.	PATC	397.6	390.3	7.3	422.0	445.0	-23.0	448.0	448.0	0
3.	PRC	421.0	448.0	-27.0	444.0	471.0	-27.0	454.0	469.0	-15
4.	MPTC	353.0	372.0	-19.0	375.0	407.0	-32.0	386.0	408.0	-22
5.	RMTC	378.0	377.0	1.0	393.0	415.0	-22.0	413.0	412.0	1
6.	CTC	416.0	414.0	2.0	449.0	462.0	-13.0	464.0	465.0	-1
7.	JTC	355.0	357.0	-2.0	378.0	399.0	-21.0	410.0	411.0	-1
8.	CRC	371.0	370.0	1.0	385.0	417.0	-32.0	411.0	424.0	-13
9.	DCTC	380.0	381.0	-1.0	406.0	410.0	-4.0	417.0	418.0	-1
10.	ATC	376.0	378.0	-2.0	409.0	435.0	-26.0	420.0	428.0	-8
11.	KTC	365.0	374.0	-9.0	385.0	410.0	-25.0	410.0	425.0	-15
12.	NTC	394.0	399.0	-5.0	417.0	424.0	-7.0	424.0	436.0	-12
13.	TPTC	404.0	397.0	7.0	421.0	421.0	0	441.0	441.0	0
14.	TTC	341.1	344.0	-2.9	360.0	374.0	-14.0	360.0	378.0	-18
15.	ASTC	—	—	—	417.0	419.0	-2.0	443.0	442.0	1
	Average	391.9	399.2	-7.3	421.0	442.0	-21.0	436.0	444.0	-8.0

Source: The Performance of Tamil Nadu STUs from 1976-77 to 1988-89, Madras: Chairman's Cell, Transport Department, Government of Tamil Nadu, pp. 45 and 56.

TABLE 2.13

Quality of Service of TNSTUs

Year	*1976-77*	*77-78*	*78-79*	*79-80*	*81-82*	*81-82*	*82-83*	*83-84*	*84-85*	*85-86*	*86-87*	*87-88*	*88-89*
No. of Break Downs per 10,000 lakh kms	1.48	1.04	1.00	0.08	0.64	0.61	0.61	0.53	0.43	0.32	0.25	0.28	0.32
No. of Accidents per 1 lakh kms	0.97	1.03	1.06	1.10	0.91	1.04	0.94	0.97	0.62	0.59	0.50	0.50	0.33

Source: The Performance of Tamil Nadu STUs from 1976-77 to 1988-89, Madras: Chairman's Cell, Transport Department, Government of Tamil Nadu, p. 36.

years of the study period, it has been around 0.5 per lakh km, which is marginally less than the average accident rate of all STUs in India which is 0.57 per lakh kms.[15] It is noted that PTC recorded high rate of accident, which is around 3 per lakh kms, except in the year 1986-87 and 1988-89, when it was 1.08 for both the years.

With regard to the number of public complaints, it is observed that TTC received the highest number of complaints from the public, which was 0.3 per lakh passengers followed by TPTC (0.15) in the year 1987-88 and in 1988-89 also TTC has received the highest number of complaints followed by NTC 0.2 per lakh passengers. Even though the rate of public complaints regarding the operations of TNSTCs has been less in number, much is to be done in the area of passenger service, passenger-crew relationship and handling of luggage.

7. DATA ENVELOPMENT ANALYSIS

Central Institute of Road Transport, Pune has developed a methodology known as Data Envelopment Analysis Technique (DEA Technique), which would eliminate imbalancing factors and try to identify the physical resources (Inputs) to be compared with Physical Output. The main resources (Input) are identified as: (i) Capital Invested, (ii) Manpower employed, (iii) Fleet of buses utilised, and (iv) Material consumed.

The total passengers served or service availed of by the travelling public is considered as Output. As every passenger has different lead or distance travelled, scientifically the passengers km has been considered as Output.

The DEA Index for the STUs of Tamil Nadu, Andhra Pradesh, Gujarat, Karnataka, Maharashtra and Uttar Pradesh has been worked out by the CIRT, Pune for the year 1989-90, which has been exhibited in Table 2.14. DEA Index reveals that Tamil Nadu Transport Corporations stood first in this regard followed by Andhra Pradesh and Gujarat. Thus, Tamil Nadu STUs have fared well in all respects.

TABLE 2.14

Data Envelopment Index for different STUs in India

Sl. No.	Description	*Andhra Pradesh SRTC*	*Gujarat SRTC*	*Karnataka SRTC*	*Maharashtra SRTC*	*Uttar Pradesh SRTC*	*Tamil Nadu Tr. Corpns.*
1	2	3	4	5	6	7	8
(A)	**Input:**						
1.	Vehicle						
	(a) Total Carrying Capacity						
	(i) Avg. Vehicles held	12646	7838	8686	14161	8010	10745
	(ii) Carrying Capacity per bus (C.C.)	55.07	72.20	59	66.04	54.00	67.38
	(iii) Buses held × C.C.	696415	565904	512474	935192	432540	723998
	(b) Eff. bus kms (lakhs)	13679	7849	8271.38	12814.19	6507.35	14732.22
2.	Manpower No. of persons employed	104986	50840	54769	105739	58541	78951
3.	Materials: Cost of Materials (Rs. in lakhs)	20775.22	11027.86	13286.88	22765.00	10366.33	24286.32
(B)	**Output:**						
	Passenger kms. (in crores)	5725.10	3307.14	3403.4	5417.61	2311.72	6783.30

(*Contd.*)

TABLE 2.14 (*Contd.*)

1	2	3	4	5	6	7	8
(C)	**Resources used per Crores Pass. kms**						
	(i) Carrying Capacity (No.)	121.64	171.12	150.58	172.61	187.11	106.73
	(ii) Effective kms (in lakhs)	2.39	2.37	2.43	2.37	2.81	2.17
	(iii) Employees (No.)	18.34	15.37	16.09	19.52	25.32	11.64
	(iv) Cost on Materials (in lakhs)	3.63	3.33	3.9	4.20	4.48	3.58
(D)	**Index for each resource (Minimum=100)**						
	(i) Carrying Capacity	114	160	141	162	175	100
	(ii) Effective km.	110	109	112	109	129	100
	(iii) Employees	158	132	138	168	218	100
	(iv) Materials	109	100	117	126	135	108
	Overall Index	491	501	508	565	557	408
(E)	**D.E. Index =** $\frac{400 \times 100}{\text{O.I.}}$	81.47	79.84	78.74	70.80	60.88	98.04
	Rank	II	III	IV	V	IV	I

DEI workings shown in Appendix II.

Source: Working Paper, CIRT: Pune.

8. SUMMARY

Bus transport has come to occupy a pivotal position in the overall transport system in India, where both private and public sectors co-exist. However, in the recent years, the share of STUs are in the decreasing order. With regard to the performance of all STUs in India, it is satisfactory in terms of fleet utilization, capital productivity, labour productivity, conservation of fuel and quality of service. But in the sphere of financial performance, it has not been satisfactory, where the losses are in the increasing order. According to the transport economists and experts including that of Planning Commission of India, these losses are not the sign of inefficiency of STUs but due to the external factors such as high incidence of taxation and depreciation and low rate of fare which are beyond the control of the STUs.

The performance of STUs in Tamil Nadu has been extremely good in respect of all the parameters of physical and operational performance and they are well above the all India STUs averages. Certain corporations are the forerunners with regard to certain performance such as fleet utilization, km efficiency, fuel conservation and bus-staff ratio. However, the financial performance has not been uniformly good. The above stated external reasons may be applied to TNSTUs also for the unsatisfactory financial performance.

Notes and References

1. Singh, Mohinder and Kadiyali, L.R., "Crises in Road Transport", 1990, Delhi: Konark Publishers Pvt. Ltd., p. 44.
2. Patankar, P.G., "Modern Trends in STUs", *JTM*, Oct. 1989, Pune: CIRT, p. 6.
3. Gandhi, Jegadish, P., 'Passenger Road Transport: Privatisation a Panacea', *Financial Express*, Sept. 20, 1991, p. 9.
4. Improvement in STUs, 1990, Pune: CIRT, p. 3.
5. Performance Statistics of STUs, 1980-81 to 1989-90, Pune: CIRT.
6. Proceedings of National Seminar on the Role of Nationalised Road Transport Undertakings, organised by the Association of State Road Transport Undertakings, New Delhi, 1990, p. 4.
7. Perumalswamy, "Economic Development of Tamil Nadu", 1990, New Delhi: S. Chand & Company, pp. 221-22.
8. Review of State Public Sector Enterprises in Tamil Nadu, 1989-90,

Madras: State Bureau of Public Enterprises (Finance Department), Government of Tamil Nadu.

9. Review of Performance of STUs (1990), Pune: CIRT, p. 4.
10. 'The Hindu', August 28, 1992, p. 3.
11. Review of State Public Sector Enterprises in Tamil Nadu, 1989-90, Madras: State Bureau of Public Enterprises (Finance Department), Government of Tamil Nadu, p. 5.
12. The Performance of Tamil Nadu State Transport Undertakings from 1976-77 to 1988-89, Madras: Chairman Cell, Transport Department, Government of Tamil Nadu, pp. 45 and 56.
13. The performance of TNSTCs, 1990, Madras: Chairman Cell, Transport Department, Government of Tamil Nadu.
14. Performance Statistics of STUs 1989, Pune: CIRT, p. 4.
15. *Ibid.*

3

Performance of Public Sector Transport: A Case Study of PATC

1. INTRODUCTION

In this chapter an attempt has been made to study the performance of PATC Ltd., from the year 1982-83, the year of its establishment to the year 1989-90, so as to understand its operational performance. The data pertaining to the first year 1982-83 has been only for a period of four months, i.e. from its inception of 1st December, 1982 to 31 March, 1983.

2. EMERGENCE OF PATC

In consonance with the State Government's policy of bringing the entire network of passenger transport under public sector, 16 corporations were established in Tamil Nadu. The Pattukottai Azhagiri Transport Corporation Ltd., (PATC) was the 9th corporation established on 1st December, 1982 to serve the entire area in North Arcot, western part of South Arcot and Northern part of Chengai M.G.R. districts with headquarters at Vellore and 16 depots, spread over its operational area. The 17th depot at Arcot was added in November 1988, by bifurcating Konavattam depot. All the 17 depots are now connected with

EXHIBIT 5

Operational Area of PATC Limited (North Arcot Region)

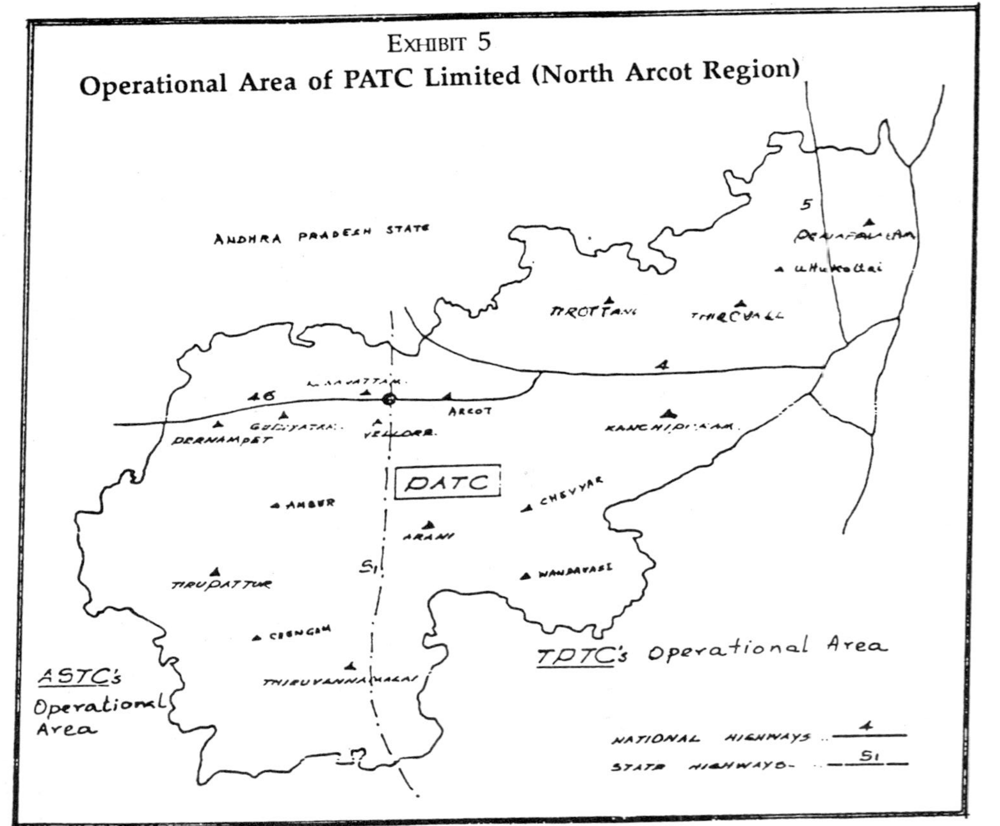

wireless sets for an effective control over its operations especially to coordinate accident relief measures, break-down service, supply of spare parts and monitor the operation of special buses during festival season. Computerisation has been introduced in all accounting transactions and for monitoring passenger traffic and movement. Pursuing the path of Cheran, Kattabomman and Nesamony Transport Corporations, PATC also started a driving school in the year 1984. It is pertinent here to mention that PATC has bagged the National Productivity Award for its best performance among the STUs in India for two consecutive years 1986-87 and 1987-88 (sixth and seventh years of its operation), which is an ample proof for its best performance.

3. EVALUATION PARAMETERS

In order to have a meaningful analysis of the performance of PATC, parameters of evaluation are discussed below under the following five headings: (i) Physical Performance, (ii) Financial performance, (iii) Personnel Management, (iv) Quality of Service, and (v) Social Responsibility.

4. PHYSICAL PERFORMANCE

The parameters of the physical performance of PATC are discussed in this section.

1. Fleet Strength

Size of a transport corporation largely depends on its fleet strength. The number of fleet denotes its size of operation. Higher the number larger is the size. Thus the growth can be measured by the increase in the number of fleets that the corporation owns.

PATC commenced its operations with 531 buses in the year 1982. At the end of the financial year the number of fleet increased to 578 (Table 3.1). The fleet strength increased to 1051 in the year 1989-90. Thus 473 buses were added during the period of study. It has also been observed that the increase of fleet has been found in all the years during the study period except during the years 1983-84 and 1988-89, where there has been a marginal decrease over the previous years.

TABLE 3.1

Fleet Strength of PATC during 1982-83 to 1989-90

Sl. No.	*Year*	*Town*	*Mofussil*	*Others*	*Total*
1.	1982-83	101	381	96	578
		(17)	(66)	(17)	
2.	1983-84	154	334	84	572
		(27)	(58)	(15)	
3.	1984-85	169	348	86	603
		(28)	(58)	(14)	
4.	1985-86	221	411	97	729
		(30)	(57)	(13)	
5.	1986-87	274	470	83	827
		(33)	(57)	(10)	
6.	1987-88	304	555	117	976
		(31)	(57)	(12)	
7.	1988-89	315	498	139	952
		(33)	(52)	(15)	
8.	1989-90	350	503	198	1051
		(33)	(48)	(19)	

Source: Annual Report of PATC for the years 1982-83 to 1988-89

The fleet strength consists of Town and Mofussil and other buses. Other buses includes spare and idle buses and buses under repair. Town buses have increased by almost three and half times during the period under review, whereas the Mofussil buses during the same period have increased only by half a time. Further, it has been noted that the proportion of Town buses to Mofussil buses have been showing an increasing trend. The share of Town buses have increased from 17 per cent in 1982-83 to 33 per cent in 1989-90, whereas the Mofussil buses have decreased from 66 to 48 per cent in the corresponding period.

2. New Buses Added

The new buses added every year during the period under review has been given in Table 3.2. Over the study period, 636

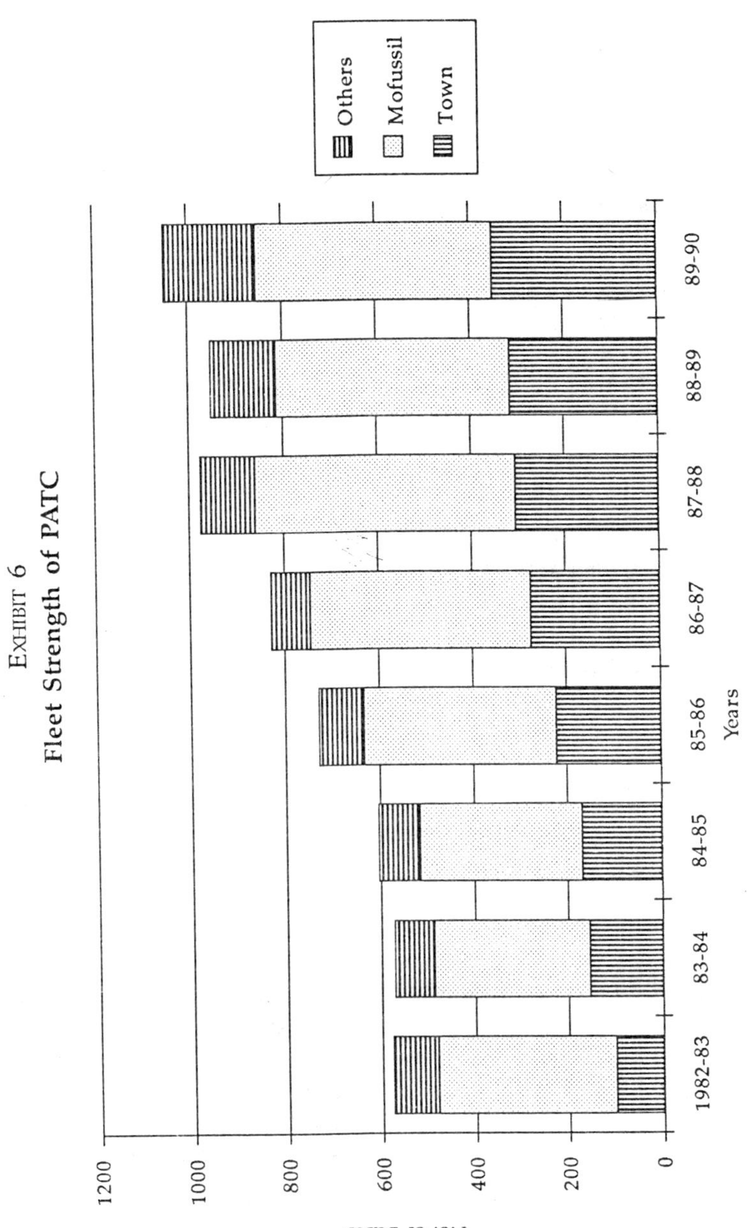

EXHIBIT 6
Fleet Strength of PATC

TABLE 3.2

Additions to Fleet Strength of PATC (1982-83 to 1989-90)

Sl. No.	*Year*	*Replacement*	*Augmentation*
1.	1982-83		—
2.	1983-84	59	1
3.	1984-85	71	29
4.	1985-86	88	107
5.	1986-87	83	101
6.	1987-88	154	67
7.	1988-89	80	23
8.	1989-90	80	23

Source: Annual Reports of PATC for the years 1982-83 to 1988-89.

buses have been replaced and 405 buses have been added. More number of replacement of buses have been due to the reason that PATC was established by converting Pallavan Transport Corporation (District Service) and transferring the buses that had been already in use for some years. The augmentation has been taking place for introducing new routes as well as operating additional services in the existing routes.

3. Age of the Buses

New buses have more advantage than the older ones. They attract the commuters and enhance their satisfaction, lighten the stress on the part of the crew members and give more kilometres per litre of diesel than the older ones. New model and technology such as aero dynamics can also be introduced. Besides, new ones cause less pollution, succumb to less number of break-downs and involve lower expenditure on repairs and maintenance than the others. Thus young buses are more favoured than the old ones. There is also a policy, in all the State Transport Corporations in Tamil Nadu, that every bus has to be replaced after 7 lakh Kms run or 6 years run whichever is earlier.

An attempt has been made to study the average age of

TABLE 3.3

Average Age of Fleet and Fleet Utilisation in PATC (1982-83 to 1989-90)

Sl. No.	*Year*	*Average Age (Years)*	*Fleet Utilisation (Percentage)*
1.	1982-83	3.78	91.1
2.	1983-84	3.73	88.9
3.	1984-85	3.73	91.4
4.	1985-86	3.18	92.0
5.	1986-87	3.01	92.2
6.	1987-88	2.84	91.2
7.	1988-89	3.00	90.9
8.	1989-90	2.95	92.1

Source: Annual Reports of PATC for the years 1982-83 to 1988-89.

buses in PATC. Table 3.3 reveals that the average age of buses range between 2.84 and 3.78 years. The average age has been in the decreasing order during the first 6 year period. From 3.78 years in the first year of its establishment it has come down to 2.84 in the sixth year. In the seventh year it has marginally increased by 0.16 years and in the last year of the study period it has declined to 2.95 years. The relatively higher age during the first four years period may be attributed again to the fact that PATC had acquired buses, which were already in use, from PTC (District Service). It has been noted that during the recent years efforts have been made by PATC to keep its buses as young as possible by replacing old buses.

4. Fleet Utilisation

It is estimated that 80 per cent of the capital employed by the Transport Corporation has been invested in the buses. Thus the higher the utilisation of buses, the higher the utilisation of the capital employed and *vice versa*.

Fleet utilisation is the ratio between the total fleet strength and the number of fleet put to use. The fleet utilisation percentage for PATC has been above 90 per cent in all the years under review, except in the year 1983-84, when it was 88.9 per cent (Table 3.3). The maximum utilisation at 92.1 per cent has been observed in the last year of the study period.

5. Number of Passengers Carried

The ultimate object of any Transport Undertaking is the mobility of the passengers. In other words, the number of passengers carried by the bus service can be taken as a measure of evaluating the performance of the transport service.

The number of passengers carried by PATC has been shown in Table 3.4. PATC has served 817.25 lakh passengers at the end of the second year of its establishment, i.e. 1983-84, from which it has grown up to 2433.19 lakh in 1989-90, recording an increase of about 3 times. Similarly, the average number of passengers travelling in a day has also doubled over the study period from 3.32 lakhs in 1982-83 to 6.68 lakhs in 1989-90. It is noted that the fleet strength has doubled during the study period, whereas the passengers served has increased by 3 times, revealing that PATC is capable of meeting the ever growing demand for mobility of the public from one place to another.

6. Number of Routes Operated

Number of passengers carried may be a criterion to know the volume of operations of transport undertaking, but one has to remember that the real service depends on making available the service to all the people who live far and wide in the area of its operation. This may be measured by the number of routes in which the corporation operates its service. Increase in the number of fleet indicates vertical growth of the transport undertaking and the number of routes may indicate the horizontal growth. Moreover, the more number of routes operated indicates, well knitted service and coverage of wider geographical area.

Table 3.5 shows the growth of routes operated by PATC during the period under review. PATC started its service with 298 routes which has increased to 585 routes in the year 1989-90, indicating that the number of routes has almost doubled over the period of 8 years of its operation. PATC operates two types of routes viz. (i) Town routes, and (ii) Mofussil routes.

TABLE 3.4

Number of Passengers Carried by PATC (1982-83 to 1989-90)

Sl. No.	Year	Number of Passengers Travelled (in Lakhs)	
		Total	Average Per Day
1.	1982-83	302.50	3.32
2.	1983-84	817.25	2.23
3.	1984-85	880.15	2.41
4.	1985-86	1419.65	3.89
5.	1986-87	1829.30	5.01
6.	1987-88	2064.52	5.80
7.	1988-89	2243.52	6.28
8.	1989-90	2433.19	6.68

Source: Annual Reports of PATC for the years 1982-83 to 1988-89.

Both these routes have shown increasing trend over the study period. However the increase in town routes have been significant, recording an increase of three and half times whereas mofussil services have recorded a marginal increase of 33 per cent.

TABLE 3.5

Number of Routes Operated by PATC (1982-83 to 1989-90)

Sl. No.	Year	Number of Routes		
		Town	Mofussil	Total
1.	1982-83	85 (29)	213 (71)	298
2.	1983-84	129 (42)	178 (58)	307
3.	1984-85	141 (43)	187 (57)	328
4.	1985-86	188 (47)	209 (53)	397
5.	1986-87	234 (49)	239 (51)	473
6.	1987-88	257 (50)	260 (50)	517
7.	1988-89	269 (50)	270 (50)	539
8.	1989-90	302 (52)	283 (48)	585

Source: Annual Reports of PATC from 1982-83 to 1989-90.

EXHIBIT 7

Average No. of Passengers and Kilometres Per Day (PATC)

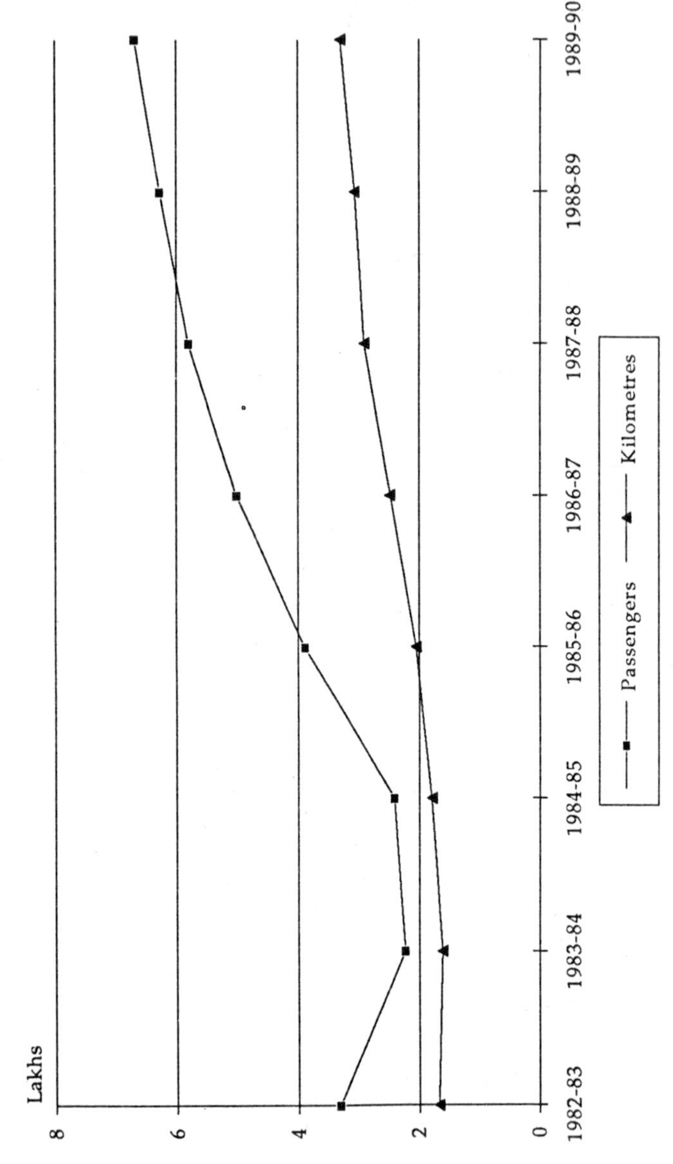

The share of Town routes in the total routes operated by PATC was only 29 per cent in the first year of operation, which increased consistently, and reached a level of 52 per cent in the year 1989-90, whereas the mofussil routes have come down from 71 per cent to 48 per cent during the same period.

7. Effective Kilometers Operated

Kilometres operated by a transport undertaking indicate on one hand the extent of utilisation of the resources viz. bus, men, etc., and on the other hand the extent of service offered for the passengers' mobility.

There has been considerable growth in the kilometre coverage by PATC. Table 3.6 shows the position regarding the kilometrage covered by PATC during the past 8 years of its existence from 1982-83. PATC has operated 578.02 lakh kms during 1983-84 which steadily increased over the years and reached a level of 1171.92 lakh kms in 1989-90, accounting for an increase by almost 2 times during the study period. This has been made possible by introducing buses in new routes as well as operating additional trips in the existing routes.

TABLE 3.6

Kilometres Operated by PATC
(1982-83 to 1989-90)

Sl. No.	*Year*	*Scheduled Kilometres (in lakhs)*	*Effective Kilometres (in lakhs)*	*Kilometre Efficiency (percentage)*
1.	1982-83	213.43	205.01	96.1
2.	1983-84	615.19	578.02	94.5
3.	1984-85	671.63	653.23	97.3
4.	1985-86	765.47	747.50	97.7
5.	1986-87	929.79	904.70	97.0
6.	1987-88	1067.62	1037.39	97.1
7.	1988-89	1128.66	1096.55	97.0
8.	1989-90	1207.50	1171.92	97.0

Source: Annual Reports of PATC for the years 1982-83 to 1988-89.

8. Kilometre Efficiency

The efficiency of the undertaking in operating their buses may be studied by another index known as kilometre efficiency. It is the ratio between the scheduled kms and operated kms and it is indicated in terms of percentage. Higher Kilometre Efficiency shows the lower cancellation of trips and/or curtailment of trips due to various reasons such as breakdowns, accidents, repair, want of crew and road blocks. Kilometre efficiency is calculated by:

$$\frac{\text{Run kilometre}}{\text{Scheduled kilometre}} \times 100$$

The km efficiency of PATC is 97 per cent (Table 3.6) in most of the years of the study period. In the first two years of its operation, it has recorded 96 and 95 per cent respectively of kilometre efficiency which shows that PATC has performed well in this regard.

9. Average Kilometre Run per Day per Bus

Utilisation of the buses can be viewed from many angles. It can be discussed in terms of distance covered by a bus per day. As already stated almost 80 per cent of the investment is made in buses. Therefore, buses must be put to use to the optimum, so as to earn maximum revenue. This can be achieved by rational crew scheduling and better maintenance of vehicles. Kilometre run by all PATC buses have been more than doubled during the study period, i.e., from 1.86 lakhs Kms. in 1982-83, it has gone upto 3.30 lakh kms (Table 3.7). The average km run per day per bus of PATC has also increased continuously in respect of Town service as well as Mofussil service.

It is indicated in Table 3.7 that the average daily kms run by all PATC buses have been more than doubled during the study period, i.e. from 1.68 lakh kms in 1982-83, it has gone upto 3.30 lakh kms. The average km run per day per bus of PATC has also increased continuously in respect of Town, Mofussil service as well as for both the services put together. The increase in the average run may be attributed to the fact that the corporation starts its operation of service early in the morning

TABLE 3.7

Average Kilometres Operated per Day per Bus (1982-83 to 1989-90)

Sl. No.	*Year*	*Average Daily km (in lakhs)*	*Average daily km Run Per Day Per Bus*		
			Town	*Mofussil*	*Overall*
1.	1982-83	1.68	274	369	349
2.	1983-84	1.62	294	366	345
3.	1984-85	1.79	310	381	358
4.	1985-86	2.05	316	393	368
5.	1986-87	2.48	322	407	376
6.	1987-88	2.91	322	410	377
7.	1988-89	3.07	323	409	377
8.	1989-90	3.30	326	419	385

Source: Annual Reports of PATC for the years 1982-83 to 1988-89.

and winds up late in nights, besides operating exclusive night services in the long routes.

10. Occupancy Ratio

This is another indicator to scale the operational efficiency of passenger transport service. It not only contributes to the revenue component of fleet operations, but also creates full employment for the bus crew and facilitates easy driving and reduces wear and tear of the accessories.

It is seen from Table 3.8, the Occupancy Ratio (OR) of Town service of PATC has been in the decreasing order. From 83.2 per cent in 1982-83 it came down to 63.4 per cent in 1984-85 and to 58.3 per cent in 1985-86 and in the last three years of the study period it is almost stagnant at 53.8 per cent. In the case of mofussil service unlike in the case of town service, it shows a better trend. However, there has been fluctuations over the years, the ratio ranging between 66.9 per cent and 83.9 per cent and in the last year of the study period it was at 80.2 per cent. The overall OR ranges between 68.9 per cent and 78.3 per cent. During the first two years it was around 69 per cent and during the next three year period it was around 75 per cent.

TABLE 3.8

Occupancy Ratio of PATC (1982-83 to 1989-90)

Sl. No.	*Year*	*Occupancy Ratio*		
		Town	*Mofussil*	*Overall*
1.	1982-83	83.2	66.9	68.9
2.	1983-84	NA	72.6	69.8
3.	1984-85	63.4	83.9	78.3
4.	1985-86	58.3	82.9	76.0
5.	1986-87	56.4	82.5	74.5
6.	1987-88	53.7	77.6	70.0
7.	1988-89	53.8	77.2	69.7
8.	1989-90	53.8	80.2	71.7

Source: Annual Reports of PATC for the years 1982-83 to 1988-89.

The ratio has again decreased and was around 70 per cent during the last three years of the study period, i.e., 1987-88 to 1989-90. The comparatively low OR in town service can be attributed to running on more uneconomic routes than that in mofussil routes, as well as running of parallel town services in mofussil routes.

11. Fuel Conservation

The STUs in India have more than 1,00,749 buses and the total consumption of HSD is about 1.6 million tonnes in 1988-89 and by the turn of the century, it would touch 4 million tonnes. The cost of HSD constitutes about 1/5 of the total cost. About 60 per cent of the material cost is on fuel and oil.[1]

It is estimated that in transport sector a 20 per cent improvement in the energy efficiency is quite possible.[2] Substantial economy can be achieved by STUs by improving fuel efficiency. The fuel efficiency is not only significant from transport undertakings' point of view but also in the nation's interest, since India's energy problem is one of demand-supply imbalance in commercial fuels as their demand has been increasing speedily while the supply has been surging sluggishly.

The fuel efficiency of bus operation is measured in terms of an index known as KMPL (kilometres obtained per litre of

TABLE 3.9

Average Kilometres per Litre of Diesel Oil in PATC (1982-83 to 1989-90)

Sl. No.	*Year*	*KMPL*		
		Town	*Mofussil*	*Overall*
1.	1982-83	3.79	3.86	3.88
2.	1983-84	3.58	3.77	3.72
3.	1984-85	3.66	3.88	3.82
4.	1985-86	3.77	3.92	3.88
5.	1986-87	3.83	3.96	3.92
6.	1987-88	3.79	3.91	3.88
7.	1988-89	3.81	3.97	3.93
8.	1989-90	3.89	4.09	4.02

Source: Annual Reports of PATC for the years 1982-83 to 1988-89.

HSD) which is the ratio of kilometres operated to the litres of HSD consumed.

It could be seen from Table 3.9 that the KMPL in PATC has increased during the study period, though there has been marginal fluctuations between the years. KMPL has increased to 3.89 and 4.09 respectively from 3.79 and 3.86 for town and mofussil services during the period of study. The overall KMPL increased from 3.88 to 4.02 during the period. It is to be noted that an all time record of 4.02 km has been there in the last year of the study period. Some of the measures taken by PATC to achieve higher fuel efficiency have been (i) Fixation of optimum speed of the vehicle, (ii) Controlling of speed by adjusting the fuel pump, (iii) Analysis of vehicle/driver-wise consumption, (iv) Fixing up targets, and (v) Rectifying and changing the course of action to achieve the target.

5. FINANCIAL PERFORMANCE

Public Transport service is quite different from other manufacturing and trading industries as its principal aim is rendering service rather than earning profits. Surplus/Deficit over the total cost of operation, average Cost of Revenue (per

Bus and per Effective kilometre operated), Ratio of Operating Cost to Operating Revenue and the Rate of Return on Capital Employed are some of the parameters of performance of public transport undertakings which are discussed below.

1. Cost and Revenue

Table 3.10 gives the financial performance to PATC during the study period 1982-83 to 1989-90. It is observed from the table that PATC has incurred loss to the extent of Rs. 97.79 lakhs during the period of 4 months in the first year 1982-83 to 1989-90 , Pune : CIRT and Rs. 151.27 lakhs in the second year. However, there was an upbeat in its financial efficiency in the subsequent three years. The surplus generated has increased from Rs. 22.12 lakhs in 1984-85 to Rs. 57.49 lakhs in 1986-87. The increase in profits was mainly on account of the benefit accrued to the PATC due to withdrawal of additional surcharge on M.V. Tax. In the year 1987-88 the corporation has again incurred heavy loss and the loss was to the tune of Rs. 243.64 lakhs. However in the next year (1988-89) itself it came out of the red and made a marginal profit of Rs. 0.6 lakh which has increased to Rs. 1.15 lakhs in 1989-90.

The loss incurred by PATC in the first two years of its operation (1982-83 and 1983-84) was due to the initial high cost

TABLE 3.10

Cost and Revenue Trends of PATC (1982-83 to 1989-90)

Year	*Total Revenue*	*Total cost* (*Rs. in lakhs*)	*Surplus/Deficits*
1982-83	566.77	664.56	(-) 97.79
1983-84	1808.22	1959.49	(-) 151.27
1984-85	2247.46	2225.34	(+) 22.12
1985-86	2865.64	2849.23	(+) 16.41
1986-87	3644.90	3587.41	(+) 57.49
1987-88	4390.17	4633.81	(-) 243.64
1988-89	4912.46	4911.86	(+) 0.60
1989-90	5487.33	5486.18	(+) 1.15

Source: Performance Statistics of STUs for the years 1982-83.

EXHIBIT 8

Revenue and Cost Trend of PATC

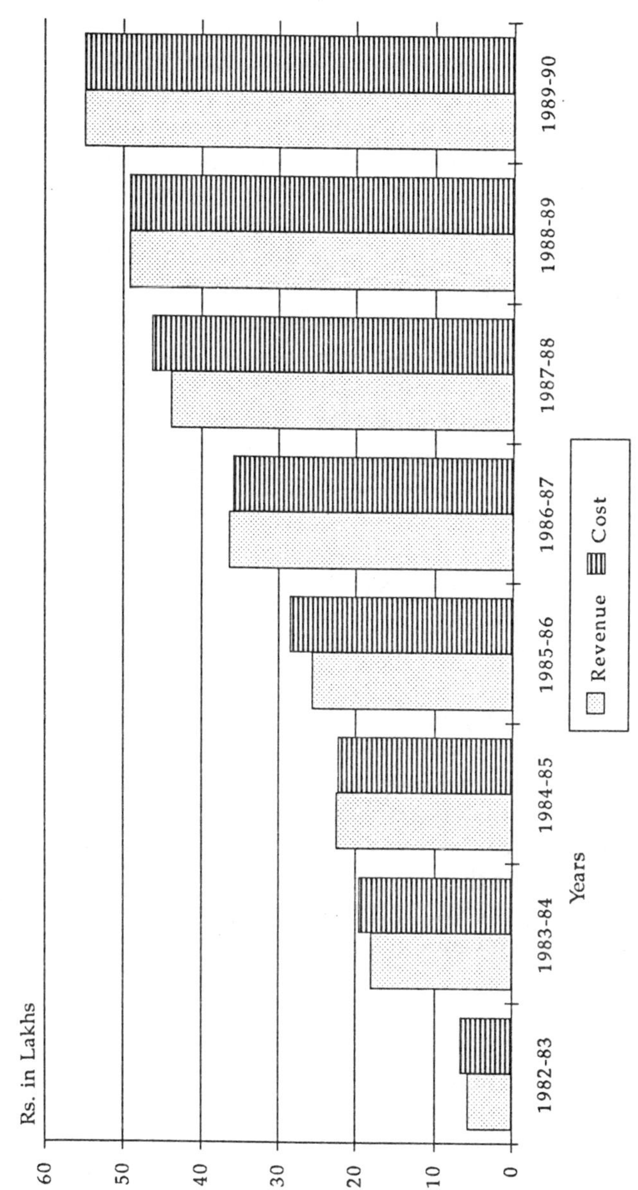

of the establishment. And the reasons for the heavy loss in 1987-88, were many. The reasons noted were stoppage of vehicles and dislocation of operation due to Vanniyar agitation and the sudden demise of the then Chief Minister of Tamil Nadu which caused a lot of disruption in the services and damage to the buses. Further during the year, expenses had increased considerably in addition to the normal growth rate commensurate with the increase in the volume of business, due to the factors such as: (i) increased M.V. Tax commitment with effect from 1st April 1987, (ii) increased provision towards depreciation on the fixed assets, (iii) increased cost of establishment due to the full year impact of the wage settlement arrived at in that year, and (iv) increase due to cost escalation of various inputs.

2. Cost and Revenue per Bus and per Effective Kilometre

In order to throw more light on the cost and revenue trend of PATC, the average cost and revenue per bus and per effective kilometre have been worked out and shown in Table 3.11.

It is observed that the average revenue per bus was Rs. 1,037 in 1982-83, which increased to Rs.1783 in 1989-90. The average cost per bus for the respective years have been Rs.1120 and Rs. 1,783. Similar trend has been observed in the case of revenue (EPKM) and cost per effective kilometre (CPKM) also. The revenue per effective km was 295.7 paise in the year 1982-83 which has increased to 468.3 paise in 1989-90 and the cost for the relative years has been 319.3 and 468.2 paise. A comparison of the average cost and revenue per bus over the period reveals that the revenue has increased by 72 per cent and cost by 59 per cent. It is to be noted that the PATC was able to increase the revenue relatively more than the cost during the study period.

3. Operating Ratio

Operating ratio is an important index for measuring the financial performance of public utilities like transport organisation. The operating Ratio is defined as :

$$\frac{\text{Operating cost}}{\text{Operating revenue}} \times 100$$

TABLE 3.11

Average Cost and Revenue Per Bus and Per Km (1982-83 to 1989-90)

Year	*Per Bus (Rs.)*			*Per Effective (Paise)*		
	Revenue	*Cost*	*Surplus/ Deficit*	*Revenue*	*Cost*	*Surplus/ Deficit*
1982-83	1037	1120	-83	295.7	319.3	-23.6
1983-84	1015	1100	-85	304.6	330.1	-25.5
1984-85	1234	1222	+12	344.1	340.7	+3.4
1985-86	1412	1404	+08	383.4	381.2	+2.2
1986-87	1518	1494	+24	402.9	396.5	+6.4
1987-88	1552	1638	-86	423.2	446.7	-23.5
1988-89	1674	1674	0	447.9	447.8	+0.1
1989-90	1783	1783	0	468.3	468.2	+0.1

Source: Performance Statistics of STUs for the years 1982-83 to 1989-90, Pune: CIRT.

Operating Cost

Though all cost such as material, labour, tax, interest and other costs can ultimately be traced to operations and classified as operating costs, it is useful to distinguish two costs viz., interest charges and taxes. Interest is a financial cost and therefore it is not an element of operating cost. Similarly, taxes such as M.V. Tax and Passenger Tax, differ from State to State due to differences in the Government concerned. It has been established that for two STUs operating under similar conditions of costs and levels of efficiency, taxes vary so much that the final profit of the organisations can be significantly different. Therefore, for the purpose of computing the operating ratio, interest and tax may be excluded.

TABLE 3.12

Operating Cost and Revenue of PATC (1982-83 to 1989-90)

Year	*Operating Cost (Rs. in lakhs)*	*Operating Revenue (Rs. in lakhs)*	*Ratio of Operating Cost to Operating Revenue (percentage)*
1982-83	1598.59	1783.94	89.6
1983-84	1629.17	1778.27	91.6
1984-85	1862.21	2198.57	84.70
1985-86	2376.30	2821.67	84.6
1986-87	3026.65	3575.96	84.6
1987-88	3907.65	4219.92	92.6
1988-89	4137.18	4763.45	86.9
1989-90	4651.72	5355.12	86.9

Source: Performance Statistics of STUs for the years 1982-83 to 1989-90, Pune: CIRT.

Operating Revenue

All the sources under which a bus operator gets his income are classified into traffic and non-traffic sources. The former includes the passenger fares, freight, receipt from contract and tourist bus service and reservation fees; while the later includes the proceeds from publicity and advertisement, royalty from canteens and stalls, sale proceeds of obsolete buses and spares and other receipts like interest and dividends on the investment of surplus funds. Though the sources are many, fare from the passengers is the main source of income of a bus operator as the earnings from all other traffic and non-traffic sources are meagre.

It is observed from Table 3.12 that the operating ratio widely fluctuates during the study period. However, it may be noted that the ratio has been less than 100 in each year denoting that the cost of service is met from the revenue. This is quite an inspiring performance of PATC, though the financial performance on the basis of total expense and revenue is not uniformly healthy (Table 3.10).

4. Rate of Return on Investment

Return on Investment is another ratio which indicates the financial performance of an undertaking. It is calculated by dividing the profit before interest by total investment. It is usually denoted in percentage.

It is noted from Table 3.13, that ROI is fluctuating. It ranges from -15.89 (1987-88) to +21.48 (1988-89) per cent. The negative rate of return has been observed in the first 2 years and in the sixth year (1986-87) of its operation. During the rest of the years, it has been above 12 per cent. In the last year of the study period, i.e., 1989-90, it has shown a profit of 20.5 per cent which is well above the minimum Rate of Return prescribed for State-owned Transport enterprises (7 per cent).[3]

The overall financial performance of PATC is satisfactory though it has not made profit uniformally in all the years of its operation. The most of the reasons for the loss are beyond the control of PATC. It is worth mentioning here the words of Planning Commission in regard to the losses of STUs, which may be attributed to PATC also, "financial viability of SRTUs has been seriously impaired by inflexible fares, and environment of rising costs, concessional travel, uneconomic routes and above all high level of taxation, periodic increases in prices of key inputs have pushed up the cost of vehicle manufacture the burden of which has been passed on to the undertakings. The position has come to such a state that unless these undertakings are

TABLE 3.13

Rate of Return on Capital of PATC
(1982-83 to 1989-90)

Sl. No.	*Year*	*% of Return*
1.	1982-83	(-) 11.89
2.	1983-84	(-) 12.99
3.	1984-85	(+) 12.37
4.	1985-86	(+) 12.20
5.	1986-87	(+) 18.50
6.	1987-88	(-) 15.8
7.	1988-89	(+) 21.48
8.	1989-90	(+) 20.50

Source: Performance Statistics of STUs for the years 1982-83 to 1989-90, Pune: CIRT.

supported with lower taxes and given the flexibility to adjust fares to match their costs, they may become a serious burden on the economy".

6. PERSONNEL MANAGEMENT

Road Passenger transport industry is highly labour-intensive and the operative staff are the backbone of the transport undertakings, through whom the revenue is being raised. Moreover, they play a crucial role in building a good image for the organisation.

1. Operative Staff

Table 3.14 shows the number of operative staff of PATC, which has been consistently increasing over the study period. From the staff strength of 3623 in the first year of its operation, its strength has increased to 6536 operative staff in 1989-90, recording an increase of 80 per cent.

2. Vehicle-Man Ratio

This ratio explains the number of employees engaged to

TABLE 3.14

Operating Staff of PATC (1982-83 to 1989-90)

Sl. No.	*Year*	*Total Operative Staff*	*Men/Bus Ratio*	*Absenteeism %*
1.	1982-83	3623	6.8	—
2.	1983-84	4113	7.7	4.5
3.	1984-85	4203	8.13	6.9
4.	1985-86	4701	7.58	5.1
5.	1986-87	5505	7.0	4.74
6.	1987-88	6068	6.9	4.49
7.	1988-89	6332	7.04	4.71
8.	1989-90	6536	6.96	4.25

Source: Performance Statistics of STUs for the years 1982-83 to 1989-90, Pune: CIRT.

operate a bus. By dividing the average number of employees per day with the average number of scheduled buses per day, VMR is calculated. A declining VMR is indicative of better performance.

The data in Table 3.14 reveal that VMR in PATC ranges between 6.8 and 8.13, the former was in the first year of its operation, i.e. 1982-83 and the latter was in the third year of its establishment (1983-84). In the last year of the study period (1989-90) it has been brought down to 6.96. It is to be noted here that in all the years of its operation the VMR of PATC has been well below the norm of 9 persons per bus prescribed by the All India Association of Road Transport Undertakings. Absenteeism percentage of the workers has also been satisfactory. The rate of absenteeism has also been less than 5 per cent during the study period except in the years 1984-85 and 1985-86 when the rate recorded was 6.9 and 5.1 per cent respectively.

3. Labour Incentives

According to the World Bank Report mush of the success of Cheran Transport Corporation (CTC) in Tamil Nadu must be attributed to the incentives given to the staff that are common among private transport competitions.[4] In the following section an attempt has been made focus on the quantum of various incentives given by PATC to its employees.

Apart from the statutory entitlements like annual Bonus, Gratuity and Provident Fund along with other usual labour welfare expenses, the employees of PATC are entitled to have Collection Batta, Collection Bonus and Performance Incentives.

Collection Batta is a percentage of the daily collections given to the crew members. The amount of collection Batta is in the increasing order during the study period. From Rs. 19.17 lakhs (Table 3.15), in 1983-84 it shot upto Rs. 34.24 lakhs recording an increase of 79 per cent during the above period.

Collection Bonus is paid to the non-crew members in all depots. There is an increasing trend in collection bonus for the past eight years totaling Rs. 620.99 lakhs (Table 3.15). From Rs. 43.97 lakhs in 1983-84 it has increased to Rs. 133.02 lakhs in 1989-90. The increase has been about three times during this period.

Performance Incentive is awarded during the strike free

TABLE 3.15

Financial Incentives to PATC Staff (1982-83 to 1989-90)

Sl. No.	*Year*	*Collection Batta (Rs. in lakhs)*	*Collection Batta (Rs. in lakhs)*	*Performance Incentive*
1.	1982-83	6.51	14.43	3.84
2.	1983-84	19.17	43.97	11.74
3.	1984-85	20.86	55.72	12.96
4.	1985-86	21.91	71.05	11.42
5.	1986-87	26.68	89.15	18.75
6.	1987-88	30.06	103.32	24.34
7.	1988-89	30.53	111.35	27.70
8.	1989-90	34.24	133.02	29.74
	Total	189.96	620.99	140.49

Source: Annual Reports of PATC for the years 1982-83 to 1989-90.

period to all the employees. Except in the year 1985-86, the Performance Incentives awarded to PATC employees have been consistently increasing over the study period, from Rs. 11.74 lakhs (Table 3.15) in 1983-84, to Rs. 29.74 lakhs recording an increase of one and half a time during the last 7 years of its operation. This reflects the cordial relationship between the workers and the management of PATC.

Apart from Collection Batta, drivers with accident free record are being given awards regularly. The relation between the staff and management continues to be cordial in all the years of the study period. Subsidised meals and tea are being provided to all the employees of the Corporation.

7. QUALITY OF SERVICE

Quality of service is one of the parameters of evaluation of the performance of a transport corporation, besides the physical and financial parameters. The parameters selected to reflect the quality of service are: 1. Break-down, 2. Accidents, and 3. Public complaints.

1. Break-downs

Break-downs, not only create unpleasant experience to the commuters, but also prove to be very costly to the operator as the buses damaged have to be made roadworthy again. Proper fleet maintenance can avoid break-downs considerably.

It is observed from Table 3.16 that the number of break-downs has been fluctuating over the study period. Maximum number of break-downs occurred in the year in 1983-84. In the year 1989-90, break-downs have come down to 3348 from 5120 in 1988-89, recording a decline of 63 per cent. Break-down per 10,000 kms is on the decreasing trend, though there have been some fluctuations during the period. In the last year of the study, it has been brought down significantly to 0.29, an all time low figure during the study period.

Break-down services are as important as preventing break-down itself. The prevailing practice of break-down service by PATC is to ask the passengers to board the next bus of their Corporation as well as other corporations, which passes through

TABLE 3.16

Number of Break-downs in PATC (1982-83 to 1989-90)

Sl. No.	*Year*	*Number of break-downs*	
		Actual	*Per 10,000 kms*
1.	1982-83	1602	0.79
2.	1983-84	6026	1.02
3.	1984-85	3652	0.56
4.	1985-86	3167	0.42
5.	1986-87	3075	0.34
6.	1987-88	4381	0.42
7.	1988-89	5120	0.46
8.	1989-90	3348	0.29

Source: Performance Statistics of STUs for the years 1982-83 to 1989-90, Pune: CIRT.

the same route, provided they stop. In the case of private buses, the crew members put the passengers in another private bus which passes through that route or refund the fare for the remaining distance to the passengers so that the passengers need not wait for another private bus to come. They can very well continue their journey by the next bus whether it is private or corporation bus. The private bus crew use their discretion, according to the situation. The PATC management can also contemplate to adopt this method.

2. Accidents

Any amount of service provided by the bus undertaking in terms of punctuality, regularity and break-down free service will be considered as nothing, if the bus meets with accident. Though there are many factors that contribute for the occurrence of accidents, most of which are beyond the control of the undertaking, the ultimate loss and responsibility is to be borne by the undertaking. So utmost care has to be exercised to prevent accidents.

Table 3.17 reveals the number of accidents in actual terms as well as the average per one lakh kilometres run. The maximum

TABLE 3.17

Accidents of PATC Buses
(1982-83 to 1989-90)

Sl. No.	*Year*	*No. of Accidents*	
		Total	*Per 1 lakhs kms*
1.	1982-83	145	0.52
2.	1983-84	370	0.46
3.	1984-85	415	0.54
4.	1985-86	525	0.55
5.	1986-87	627	0.41
6.	1987-88	608	0.43
7.	1988-89	575	0.39
8.	1989-90	587	0.34

Source: Performance Statistics of STUs for the years 1982-83 to 1989-90, Pune: CIRT.

number of accidents occurred in 1986-87 the number of accidents being 627. The number of accidents came down to 587 in the last year of the study period, i.e. 1989-90. The accidents per one lakh kms run have been on the decreasing trend from 0.55 in the year 1985-86 to 0.34 per one lakh kms in 1989-90.

3. Number of Public Complaints

Number of complaints made by the public about the operation of bus service may be an indicator that depicts the level of performance of the transport undertaking.

Number of complaints received by PATC has been in the decreasing order during the study period. Though the number of public complaints are minimum, it should be kept in mind that our tolerant national ethos might have resulted in lower number of complaints from the customers. PATC has to be responsive to commuters' feelings rather than waiting for them to complain.

8. SOCIAL RESPONSIBILITY

Performance of business enterprises is usually judged on

TABLE 3.18

Public Complaints with Regard to PATC per Lakh Passengers (1982-83 to 1989-90)

Sl. No.	*Year*	*Number of Complaints*
1.	1982-83	NA
2.	1983-84	NA
3.	1984-85	NA
4.	1985-86	NA
5.	1986-87	NA
6.	1987-88	0.02
7.	1988-89	0.03
8.	1989-90	0.02

Source: Performance Statistics of STUs for the years 1982-83 to 1989-90, Pune: CIRT.

the basis of its financial performance. However, in the case of public sector enterprises, especially public utilities such as STUs, profitability is not the sole criterion to evaluate its performance. The very purpose of state's participation through the process of nationalisation is to strengthen the economy by looking beyond the narrow boundaries of profit and loss. The social obligations undertaken by STUs may be in the form of, (i) extending their operation to hitherto unconnected villages, (ii) fare concession to students and physically handicapped persons, and (iii) operation of buses on uneconomic routes and roads.

1. Number of Villages Connected

India has more than 70 per cent of its population living in scattered rural areas. Their demand for economic, social, educational and health needs have to be met. Even after four decades of developing the transport infrastructure, nearly 36 per cent of a total of 575,936 villages are even today without any means of transportation. Private bus operators can hardly be expected to play significant role in this task for obvious reasons, nor the railways because of the fixity of terminal routes. On the other hand, only nationalised passenger road transport organisations can be mandated to recognise this responsibility on behalf of government and to operate their services to meet the transport demand in remote habitats.[5]

Table 3.19 shows the number of new villages connected with nearby towns. It is observed from the table that the highest number of villages have been connected with the passenger transport network in the year 1989-90. This phenomenal growth has been due to the policy decision of the government taken during that year to provide bus facility to all villages with population of 1000 or more. Till that year, bus facilities have been extended only to the villages with population of 1500 or more. About 99 villages have been provided with bus facilities in the year 1987-88 followed by 58 villages in the year 1985-86 and 25 villages in the year 1986-87. During the rest of the years of the study period, only a few villages have been covered.

The population benefited as a result of the extension of bus facilities to the above villages, also has been increasing though there has been marginal fluctuation. In the first three years, the population benefited has been very meagre. However in the third year it was 40,000 and in the last year of study period it has increased to 2.34 lakhs.

TABLE 3.19

Number of New Villages Served by PATC Buses (1982-83 to 1989-90)

Sl. No.	*Year*	*No. of New Villages Connected*	*Population Benefited (in Lakhs)*
1.	1982-83	7	0.90
2.	1983-84	2	0.02
3.	1984-85	2	0.03
4.	1985-86	58	0.40
5.	1986-87	25	0.31
6.	1987-88	99	0.85
7.	1988-89	12	0.20
8.	1989-90	137	2.34

Source: Records of PATC form 1982-83 to 1989-90

2. Financial Commitment of PATC in Discharging Social Responsibility

PATC has been giving concessions in fares to specified categories of passengers such as students, blinds, handicaps, journalists and freedom fighters. In giving such concessions, the corporation has earmarked certain amount of revenue every year. In addition to the revenue foregone on such services, the Corporation also incurs certain additional cost on operation of buses in bad earthen or katcha roads and operation of buses in uneconomic routes. Table 3.20 indicates cost incurred by PATC on the above services. The cost of student concessions has been

TABLE 3.20

Social Obligations Undertaken by PATC (1986-87 to 1989-90)

	1986-87	*1987-88*	*1988-89*	*1989-90*
(a) Annual cost of student concession ...Rs.	244375	269752	275344	322856
(b) Annual cost of concession given to classes such as blinds, handicaps and journalists ...Rs.	132720	89724	84393	60415
(c) Total kms Operated on Bad and Earthen or Katcha Roads ...	451	580	22725	23535
(d) Estimated additional cost of operation on Bad/Earthen road ...Rs.	722	1044	40905	41132
(e) Average number of uneconomic trips operated as a social obligation per day ...	96	107	145	Nil
(f) Estimated loss incurred on account of uneconomic trips ...Rs.	4752	5671	8410	Nil
Total Financial Commitment on (a), (b), (d) and (f)	382569	366191	409052	424403

Source: Records of PATC.

consistently increasing over the study period from Rs. 2.44 lakhs in 1986-87 to Rs. 3.23 lakhs in 1989-90 recording an increase of 32 per cent over the four year period. It is interesting to note that the cost of concession given to the other categories of passengers such as blinds and handicapped has been in the decreasing order. From Rs. 1.33 lakhs in 1986-88, it has been consistently declining and come down to Rs. 0.6 lakhs in 1989-90. The reason for such decline may be due to the procedure for the issue of such concessions being too cumbersome. Another factor for such decrease may also be that the concession is given only in the town service buses. Such concessions are allowed by the private bus operators with minimum formalities and procedures and the passengers get the concessions both in the case of town and mofussil bus services.

9. DATA ENVELOPMENT ANALYSIS

The DEA Index for PATC has been worked out, taking 1983-84 as the base year. It is seen from the Table 3.21 that the performance has marginally decreased from the base year. However, it is noticed that in the last year of the study period, i.e. 1989-90, the DE Index has been 107, denoting that PATC has fared well.

10. SUMMARY

The above review of performance of Pattukottai Azhagiri Transport Corporation Ltd., reveals that there has been a substantial growth in the operation of its services. Physical performance in terms of fleet strength, number of routes, kilometres operated, fleet utilisation, occupancy ratio, KMPL have uniformly increased over the study period and its services have been well tuned to meet the mobility demand of the public by offering quality service which is reflected in the decreasing number of break-downs, accidents and public complaints. The employees' welfare too has been taken care of. There has been a well designed incentive system for different categories of employees, which aims at motivating them for greater commitment and higher productivity. However, in the financial sphere, the performance of PATC has not been uniformly good.

TABLE 3.21

Data Envelopment Analysis for PATC (1983-84 to 1989-90)

	Input	*1983-84*	*84-85*	*85-86*	*86-87*	*87-88*	*88-89*	*89-90*
I.	(a) Average Vehicles Held	530	546	604	766	883	882	922
	(i) Carrying Capacity (C.C.)	64	66	68	68	72	69	69
	(ii) Bus held XCC	33920	36036	41072	52088	63576	60858	63618
	(b) Effective Bus km (lakhs)	583.57	653.23	747.5	904.7	1037.39	1096.85	1171.92
	No. of persons employed	4414	4203	4701	5505.0	6068.0	6332.0	6878.0
	Material Cost (i) Actuals	832.39	961.91	1118.12	1463.19	1774.52	1836.95	1939.76
	(ii) at 83-84*	832.39	913.06	998.95	1207.95	1390.58	1299.12	1348.93
II.	Output							
	Passenger kms (in crores)	332.40	330.23	375.17	449.0	510.65	527.51	622.17
III.	Resources used per crore Passenger kms							
	(i) Carrying Capacity (No.)	102.04	109.12	109.48	116.00	124.50	115.37	102.25
	(ii) Effective kms (in lakhs)	1.79	1.98	1.99	2.01	2.03	2.08	1.88
	(iii) Employees (No.)	13.28	12.73	12.53	12.26	11.88	12.00	11.05
	(iv) Cost on Materials (in lakhs)	2.50	2.77	2.66	2.69	2.72	2.46	2.17

IV.	Index for each resources (1983-84=100)							
	Carrying Capacity	100	107	107	114	122	113	100
	Effective km	100	111	111	112	113	116	105
	Employees	100	96	94	92	89	90	83
	Materials Cost	100	111	106	108	109	98	87
	Overall Index	400	425	418	426	433	417	375
V.	D.E. Index = $\frac{400 \times 100}{\text{O.I.}}$	100	94	96	94	92	96	107

*Appendix III.

Source: Performance Statistics of STUs for the years 1982-83 to 1989-90, Pune: CIRT.

During the study period of eight years it has earned profit during five years to the tune of Rs. 116.6 lakhs and suffered loss during three years totalling to Rs. 539.9 lakhs. The reasons for such a huge loss have been, hike in the price of fuel, tubes and tyres, mounting staff pay bills, unremunerative fare structure, heavy taxes and large provision for depreciation and in addition bandhs and hartals which have not only taken away the revenue but also caused damages to the buses. Most of these reasons are beyond the control of PATC. The Social Responsibility discharged by the PATC in terms of number of new villages connected with bus service and population benefited has been significant. However, the concessions availed by the blind and handicapped have been in the decreasing order.

In a nutshell the performance of PATC has been remarkable. No less a body of national standing than the National Productivity Council, has recognised the outstanding performance of PATC and conferred the award for best performance twice consecutively during the years 1986-87 and 1987-88. The Data Development Analysis also reveals that PATC has been able to generate substantial output for the resources utilised.

Notes and References

1. Patankar, P.G., "Modern Trends in State Transport Undertaking", *JTM*, Oct. 1989, Pune: CIRT, p. 9.
2. Patankar, P.G., "Energy Conservation in Road Transport", *JMT*, March 1989, Pune: CIRT, p. 6.
3. Gopala Krishna, "Return for State Enterprises - I", *Financial Express*, 31st July 1992.
4. Armstrong Alan, *et al*, 1987, "Bus Services Reducing Costs, Rising Standards", World Bank Technical paper number 68, Urban Transport Series, Washington : The World Bank, p. 18.
5. Raman, A.V., "Road Transport: Case against Privatisatoin", *Financial Express*, 10th July 1989.

4

Passengers' Bus Usage Profile and Preference

1. INTRODUCTION

This chapter reviews the bus usage profile of the respondents and their preference among PATC, Private and other government Corporation buses in North Arcot Region. The review is based on primary data collected from the sample respondents using schedule. The respondents' bus usage profile and their preference have been related to their socio-economic factors.

Transport is a public utility service. A welfare government is required to monitor the development of various types of transport such as passenger transport and goods transport, so as to provide maximum service to the public. With this view, the government should formulate a passenger transport policy defining the role of the private sector. The government can delineate a role for itself in this regard. The government can enter into the passenger transport either directly playing buses in new routes not allowing private operators and also nationalising the existing private bus operation. The policy of the government relating to this aspect should entail the extent of bus operation allowed to the private sector and public sector.

In other words, the ratio between buses operated by public sector transport corporations and that allowed to the private transport operators should form part of the overall transport policy of the government. An assessment of usage of buses and preference between buses operated by government corporation and private operators by a travelling public will help deciding the sector mix in plying buses.

In this regard it is pertinent to make a region-based survey of the passengers' travel profile and their preference for buses for travel. This chapter is an attempt in this direction, so as to study the above-mentioned aspects in detail.

The chapter focuses on two broad aspects viz.,

1. The bus usage profile of the respondents.
2. Respondents' preference for PATC, Private and other Government Corporation bus operations and reasons for such preference.

The socio-economic factors influencing the bus usage profile and preference of the respondents have also been studied.

2. BUS USAGE PROFILE OF THE RESPONDENTS

A passenger normally travels in any bus which is available at the time of his journey. Therefore, it is expected that any passenger would have travelled in the buses operated by PATC, private bus operators and those run by other Government Corporations. However, there are certain routes in which PATC, private and other corporation buses have a close schedule which enable the passengers to choose or to prefer the bus for his travel. During such times the passengers exercise their preference based on their priority for speed, comfortable travel, better interaction with the bus crew, etc. The extent of such preference and usage of buses by the sample respondents have been measured in this study as explained below.

The respondents were asked to rank PATC, Private and other Transport Corporation buses in the order of their bus usage. The question put to them in this connection was

TABLE 4.1

Bus Usage Profile of the Sample Respondents

Name of the Bus operator	*No. of Respondents who have given rank*			*Weighted Scores*	*Average Weighted Score*	*Rank*
	I	*II*	*III*			
PATC	171	121	8	763	2.5	1
Private	110	158	32	678	2.3	2
Other Govt. Corporations	21	22	86	193	1.8	3

EXHIBIT 9

Bus Usage of the Respondents among PATC, Private and Others

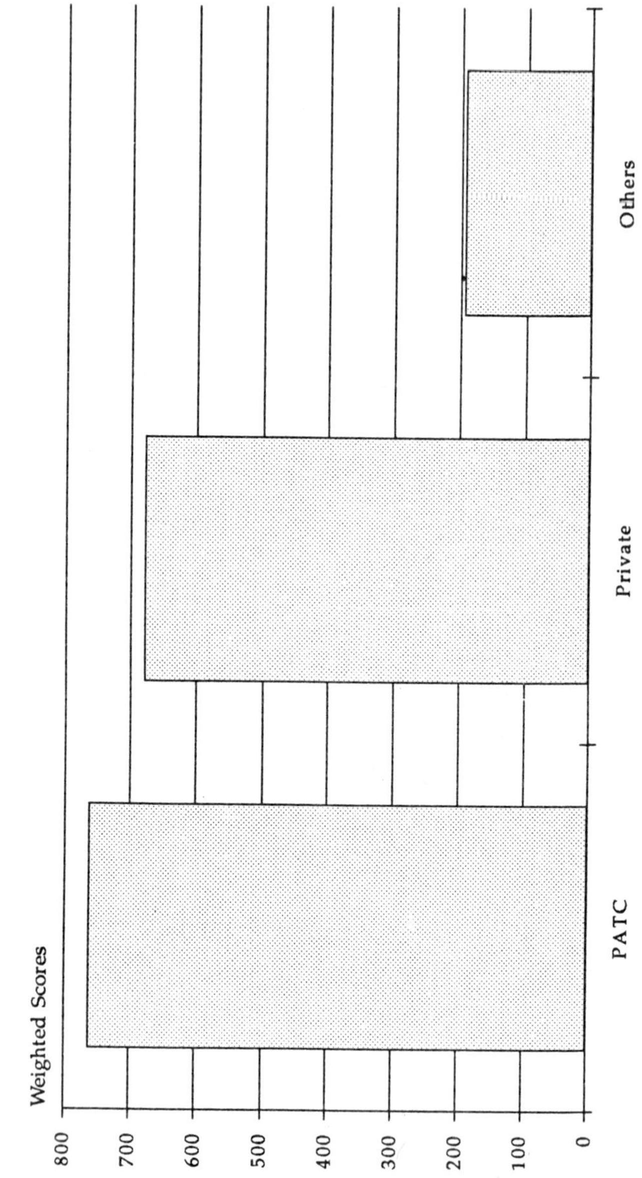

"Generally by which bus you used to travel?
(kindly rank in the order of usage)

(a) PATC (   ), (b) Private (   ), (c) Other Government Corporation (   )"

Weight is assigned to each rank given by the passengers. The first rank has been alloted 3 weights , second rank 2 weights and the third rank 1 weight. Accordingly weighted scores have been calculated, on the basis of which it has been found out which bus the respondents have mostly used for travel and the order of their usage.

The weighted scores have been arrived at as explained below. 171 respondents who have given PATC, the I rank are awarded 3 weights each. Therefore, they get a total of 513 (171 x 3) weighted scores (Table 4.1). Similarly, 121 respondents who ranked PATC II are awarded 2 weights each and their total weighted score is 242 (121 x 2). Eight respondents who have ranked PATC III are awarded 1 weight each and their total weighted score has been 8 (8 x 1). Thus PATC gets a total of 763 weighted scores from all the 300 respondents. In the same process, the weighted score for private buses has been arrived at 678 from all the 300 respondents. Only 129 have ranked other corporation buses. Perhaps they have not travelled by buses run by other corporations. One reason could be that in the routes they travel no such buses ply. The weighted score of the 129 respondents, for these buses has been arrived at 193 through the same process as already explained. The average weighted scores for the 3 groups of bus operators are thus arrived at 2.5, 2.3 and 1.5 respectively. Thus PATC gets the I rank, denoting that passenger respondents have used PATC buses more than the buses operated by the other operators. The lowest rank for other Corporation buses may be attributed to the fact that these buses plying in this region are few in number compared with that the PATC and private buses.

3. BUS USAGE PROFILE AND SOCIO-ECONOMIC FACTORS INFLUENCING BUS USAGE

In order to have more meaningful analysis of the bus

usage profile of the respondents, the socio-economic variables of the respondents have been related to their travel behaviour.

1. Residential Area of the Respondents and Bus Usage

The utilisation of a bus depends on its availability, frequency and the service it provides, which may differ from place to place. Hence an attempt has been made to study the usage profile of the rural and urban respondents. Respondents have been divided into Rural and Urban based on the place of their residence. Respondents, whose place of residence is in the town/city in which the survey has been conducted or in other taluk headquarters have been taken as Urban respondents and the rest have been taken as Rural.

Table 4.2 reveals that in the case of PATC the weighted score (438) as well as average weighted score (2.6) of the urban respondents are more than that of rural respondents. The scores are in the reverse in the case of private buses.

TABLE 4.2

Place of Residence and Bus Usage

Place of Residence	*No. of Respondents*	*Weighted Scores for bus usage*		
		PATC	*Private*	*Others*
Urban	171	438 (2.6)	373 (2.2)	126 (1.5)
Rural	129	325 (2.5)	305 (2.4)	67 (1.5)

Though both the urban and the rural passengers use PATC buses more than the private buses, among the users of PATC buses urban passengers use PATC buses more than the rural passengers.

2. Age and Bus Usage

Age is a factor closely related to the preference of the respondents to utilise a certain type of buses, as the need and priority of one age group may differ from another. Hence an effort is made to study the usage profile of the respondents of

TABLE 4.3

Age and Bus Usage

Age (Years)	*No. of Respondents*	*Weighted Scores*		
		PATC	*Private*	*Others*
Less than 25	114	281 (2.5)	265 (2.3)	73 (1.6)
25-40	131	337 (2.6)	290 (2.2)	89 (1.5)
40-55	45	122 (2.7)	100 (2.2)	23 (1.6)
Above 55	10	23 (2.3)	26 (2.6)	8 (2)

different age groups.

Respondents have been divided into four groups, based on their age as shown in Table 4.3. It is observed from the table that as the use of the respondents goes up, the usage rate for PATC also goes up upto the age group 'between 40 and 55 years' and then declines. Among the users of private buses, the score is almost stagnant (2.2) for the second and the third group. It is 2.6 for the last group. Therefore, it is inferred that the respondents of age upto 55 years travelled more by PATC buses than by private buses. Contrarily the higher age group respondents (above 55 years) have travelled more by private buses than by PATC buses.

3. Sex and Marital Status and Bus Usage

It has been attempted to identify the usage profile of the respondents based on their sex and marital status.

It is observed from Tables 4.4 and 4.5 that the weighted scores (554 and 209) as well as the average weighted scores (2.6 and 2.5) of both male and female respondents are more for PATC buses than for private buses. However among the groups, male respondents have utilised more of PATC buses than female respondents and in the case of private buses female respondents have used them more than PATC buses. It is inferred that both

TABLE 4.4

Sex and Bus Usage

Sex	*No. of Respondents*	*Weighted Scores*		
		PATC	*Private*	*Others*
Male	216	554 (2.6)	484 (2.2)	132 (1.6)
Female	84	209 (2.5)	194 (2.3)	61 (1.4)

TABLE 4.5

Marital Status and Bus Usage

Marital Status	*No. of Respondents*	*Weighted Scores*		
		PATC	*Private*	*Others*
Married	166	429 (2.6)	371 (2.2)	103 (1.5)
Un-Married	134	334 (2.5)	307 (2.3)	90 (1.6)

male and female respondents have been using PATC buses more than the private buses. Similar usage pattern has been found in case of married and unmarried respondents in the same order as that of made and female.

4. Level of Education and Bus Usage

The relationship between the bus usage profile and the level of education has been shown in Table 4.6. It is observed that the illiterate respondents are using more of private buses than PATC buses. The rest of the respondents are using PATC buses more than the private buses. Their weighted average score ranges between 2.1 and 2.7 for private buses and 2.3 and 2.6 for PATC buses.

It is inferred that all the educated respondents irrespective of their level of education have used PATC buses more than

TABLE 4.6

Level of Education and Bus Usage

Sl. No.	*Level of Education*	*No. of Respon-dents*	*Weighted Scores*		
			PATC	*Private*	*Others*
1.	Illiterates	6	14 (2.3)	16 (2.7)	2 (1)
2.	Educated upto SSLC	35	90 (2.6)	83 (2.4)	12 (1.5)
3.	Educated upto HSC	61	154 (2.5)	144 (2.4)	23 (1.5)
4.	Diploma holders	44	115 (2.6)	101 (2.3)	21 (1.4)
5.	Degree holders	86	216 (2.5)	193 (2.2)	74 (1.4)
6.	Post-graduates and Professionals	68	174 (2.6)	141 (2.1)	61 (1.6)

private buses. The illiterate respondents have used more of private buses than PATC buses.

5. Occupation and Bus Usage

The respondents have been divided into groups based on their occupation and their bus usage profile has been studied.

It is observed from Table 4.7 that the respondents who fall under the 'other occupation category' which includes agriculturists, labourers, self-employed and unemployed have been found to have utilised both PATC and private buses equally with average weighted score of 2.5 for each type of operation. In the case of 'Businessmen' and 'Students' it is observed that the usage score for both PATC buses is marginally higher than that of private buses. However, the employees in private sector seem to use more of PATC buses (2.7) than private buses, followed by employees in Government sector with the weighted average score of 2.6 and Executives in public/private sector (2.4). The weighted average score of all these three categories of employees for private buses is 2.2. It is inferred that employees in both the

TABLE 4.7

Occupation and Bus Usage

Sl. No.	*Level of Education*	*No. of Respon-dents*	*Weighted Scores for bus usage*		
			PATC	*Private*	*Others*
1.	Employees in Govt. Sector	88	231 (2.6)	192 (2.2)	67 (1.4)
2.	Employees in Private Sector	51	136 (2.7)	112 (2.2)	27 (1.5)
3.	Executives in Pvt./Govt. Sector	45	110 (2.4)	97 (2.2)	43 (1.7)
4.	Businessmen	37	92 (2.5)	87 (2.4)	19 (1.6)
5.	Students	39	94 (2.4)	90 (2.3)	29 (1.6)
6.	Others	40	101 (2.5)	100 (2.5)	8 (1)

public sector and the private sector use more of PATC buses than private buses and the other categories of respondents utilise both the private and the PATC buses almost equally.

6. Monthly Income and Bus Usage

The respondents have been grouped into three categories based on their income. 28 respondents did not receive any income and hence not included. The bus usage profile of the respondents with different levels of monthly income reveals (Table 4.8) that the second group of respondents with income ranging from Rs. 1001 to 3000 has the highest weighted score of 396, the average weighted score being 2.6 for PATC buses, followed by the third group (with income above Rs. 3000) with average weighted score of 2.5 and the average score of these two group of respondents for private buses are 2.2 and 2 respectively. In the case of the first group of respondents (with income upto Rs.1000) the weighted and average score for PATC are 184 and 2.5 and 173 and 2.4 for private buses respectively.

It is inferred that the respondents whose monthly income

TABLE 4.8

Monthly Income and Bus Usage

Sl. No.	*Monthly Income (in Rs.)*	*No. of Respon-dents*	*Weighted Scores*		
			PATC	*Private*	*Others*
1.	Upto 1000	73	184 (2.5)	173 (2.4)	34 (1.5)
2.	1001 to 3000	153	396 (2.6)	340 (2.2)	96 (1.5)
3.	Above 3000	31	78 (2.5)	62 (2)	36 (1.6)

is upto Rs.1000 travel by both PATC and private buses almost equally, whereas the respondents whose income are above Rs.1000 use PATC buses relatively more than private buses.

7. Purpose of Travel and Bus Usage

The purpose of the travel may also influence the decision of the passengers in selecting the type of bus in which he/she wants to travel. Passengers travel by buses for various purposes. Some travel to their place of work, such as offices, shops, factories, farms, hospitals, schools and other educational institutions. Some travel for buying of goods for resale, collecting bills and for going to various officers in connection with their business. A few travel in order to get certificates to seek employment and also to meet personal requirements like visiting doctors and attending social functions namely marriages and entertainments. The respondents have been asked to state the appropriate purpose for which they mostly travel, viz., social, business and official. Respondents travelling for personal purposes also have stated social. Thus the social purpose includes personal travel also.

Table 4.9 reveals that the respondents who travel for social purpose use more of PATC buses then private buses whose average weighted scores are 2.6 and 2.1 respectively.

The respondents who travel in connection with their office

TABLE 4.9

Purpose of the Travel and Bus Usage

Sl. No.	*Purpose of Travel*	*No. of Respon-dents*	*Weighted Scores*		
			PATC	*Private*	*Others*
1.	Social	106	279 (2.6)	222 (2.1)	76 (1.7)
2.	Business	44	108 (2.5)	106 (2.4)	20 (1.4)
3.	Official	150	376 (2.5)	350 (2.3)	97 (1.4)

work and business, have utilised PATC buses at the same level, whose average weighted score is 2.5 each and the average score for private bus is 2.3 for the former and 2.4 for the latter category of respondents. It is inferred that the respondents who travel for social purpose use PATC buses relatively more than the private buses, whereas respondents who take business trips utilise both PATC and private buses almost equally.

TABLE 4.10

Distance Travelled and Bus Usage

Sl. No.	*Distance Travelled per month (kms.)*	*No. of Respon-dents*	*Weighted Scores*		
			PATC	*Private*	*Others*
1.	Upto 500	157	410 (2.6)	355 (2.3)	80 (1.4)
2.	501 to 1000	65	165 (2.5)	144 (2.2)	50 (1.5)
3.	Above 1000	78	185 (2.4)	177 (2.3)	65 (1.6)

8. Distance Travelled and Usage

The relationship between distance travelled by the respondents and their usage profile is shown in Table 4.10.

It is interesting to note that the respondents who travel 'more than 1000 kms' per month on an average used both PATC and private buses almost equally. Both the group of respondents who travel 'less than 500 kms' and '501 to 1000 kms' per month on an average, tend to use relatively more of PATC buses, than private buses, regarding which the average weighted score is 2.6 for PATC and 2.3 for private buses in the former group and 2.5 and 2.2 for the latter group of respondents. It is inferred that respondents who travel more use both private and PATC buses equally and who travel less have used PATC buses more than private buses.

9. Frequency of Travel and Bus Usage

Frequency of travel may facilitate the passengers to have more knowledge of the operation of the different type of buses. Hence the study of the bus usage profile of the respondents with different level of frequencies of travel is vital for the purpose of comparing the PATC with private bus operation in the study region.

It is observed from Table 4.11 that the 'Daily Travellers' use both the private and the PATC buses equally, with the

TABLE 4.11

Frequency of Travel and Bus Usage

Sl. No.	*Frequency of Travel*	*No. of Respon-dents*	*Weighted Scores*		
			PATC	*Private*	*Others*
1.	Daily	132	322 (2.4)	317 (2.4)	81 (1.4)
2.	Frequently	87	327 (3.8)	181 (2.1)	74 (1.5)
3.	Occasionally	81	214 (2.6)	180 (2.2)	38 (1.6)

weighted average score of 2.4 for both the type of bus operation. Quite contrary to this, the 'Frequent' travellers are using more of PATC buses, than private buses,whose weighted average score for the former is 3.8 and 2.1 for the latter. The 'Occasional traveller' also uses relatively more of PATC buses than the private buses. The reason for the equal use of both PATC and private buses by the daily travellers may be the fare concession extended by the private operators and other preferences such as stopping at convenient places and offering seats to the daily travellers.

10. Owning Personal Vehicle and Usage

Meaningful inference can be drawn by studying the usage profile of the respondents who own personal vehicle, as they would be more choosy than the other respondents who do not own any vehicle. There are 28 respondents who own moped, 46 own motor cycle/scooter, 6 own car and rest of the respondents own no vehicle.

It is observed from the Table 4.12 that the weighted average score of the respondents who own motor cycle/scooter has been 2.6 for PATC and it is 2.5 for the owners of car and moped. The score for private buses has been 2.2 for all the categories of respondents who own one or the other type of vehicle, whereas, the average score for the respondents who own no vehicle has been almost equal for both PATC (2.4) and private (2.3) buses. It is inferred that the respondents owning vehicle have used more PATC buses than private buses and the respondents who do not own any vehicle have used both PATC and private buses equally.

4. PASSENGERS' PREFERENCE FOR PATC/PRIVATE BUSES

Nationalised passenger road transport in India is about four decades old. The issue of nationalisation is however, still controversial. On the one hand, the STUs have been applauded for their social considerations. On the other hand, they are vehemently criticised for their heavy loss year after year, inspite of certain advantages such as the economies of large scale operations, professional management and its limited monopolistic nature.

TABLE 4.12

Possession of Personal Vehicle and Bus Usage

Sl. No.	*Type of Vehicle*	*No. of Respon-dents*	*Weighted Scores*		
			PATC	*Private*	*Others*
1.	None	220	559 (2.4)	504 (2.3)	130 (1.5)
2.	Moped	28	69 (2.5)	62 (2.2)	23 (1.6)
3.	Motor Cycle/Scooter	46	120 (2.6)	99 (2.2)	35 (1.5)
4.	Car	6	15 (2.5)	13 (2.2)	5 (1.7)

In recent years, there has been a lot of talk on the privatisation of transport sector. The share of passenger road transport in the hands of STUs, measured in terms of fleet strength has progressively declined. Apart from the financial performance, the passenger amenities and benefits have a greater stake in deciding the mix between the private and public transport operations. Where the passenger amenities and comforts increase, the passengers' preference for such operations may also increase. Consequently, it may pave the way for more and more share for STUs operations and *vice versa*. This part of analysis aims to study the preference of respondents amongst the private and the PATC buses in North Arcot Region of Tamil Nadu, and also the reasons for such preference.

1. Passengers' Preference

Among the total respondents of 300, 15 respondents, accounting for 5 per cent have expressed that they have no special preference for any specific type of bus operation. About 61 per cent (Table 4.13) of respondents, numbering 184 have preferred PATC buses and 101 (34 per cent) have preferred private buses. It is inferred that majority of passengers prefer public sector buses.

TABLE 4.13

Passengers' Preference for PATC/Private Bus

Preference	*No. of respondents*
PATC	184 (61)
Private	101 (34)
None	15 (5)
Total	300

5. PASSENGERS' PREFERENCE AND THEIR SOCIO-ECONOMIC PROFILE

Further the respondents' preference has been studied with reference to their socio-economic background such as place of residence, age, income, etc. The following are the outcome of such analysis:

1. Passengers' Preference and their Place of Residence

Travel need largely varies from place to place. The people in urban areas may require buses to be punctual and be available more in number, whereas the people in rural areas may prefer to have buses which stop at their place of convenience willing to carry luggage at low rates. An attempt have been made to find out the preference of passengers for PATC/Private buses based on place of residence.

Of the total number of 285 passengers who have reported their preference, 164 (58 per cent) are from urban areas and 121 (42 per cent) are from rural areas. As many as 117 respondents, representing 71 per cent of urban dwellers, have preferred PATC buses, whereas only 67 respondents, accounting for 55 per cent of rural dwellers have preferred PATC buses. It is observed that though more of the urban and rural passengers have preferred PATC buses, the preference for the same was more among the urban passengers than among the rural passengers. This

TABLE 4.14

Place of Residence and Passenger Preference of Bus

Place of Residence	*No. of Respondents*		*Total*
	PATC	*Private*	
Urban	117(71)	47(29)	164
Rural	67(55)	54(45)	121
Total	184(65)	101(35)	285

Calculated χ^2=7.08 P=0.007
Table χ^2 =6.63 Significant at 1 % level

phenomenon may be due to the reasons that the rural passengers may want to have personalised service. Such service is offered more by the private bus sector than by the PATC.

In order to find out whether there is any significant relationship between the place of residence of the passengers and their preference, chi-square test has been applied for Table 4.14.

The calculated chi-square value (7.08) is more than the table value. Therefore, the relationship between the place of residence and passengers' preference is significant at 1% level.

2. Age and Preference

The preference of the respondents for PATC/Private buses was studied in relation to their age. It is observed from Table 4.15 that the respondents who are above 55 years of age have been equally divided between PATC and private buses as patrons. The respondents of other age groups have preferred PATC buses more than private buses, in which around 65 per cent of them have favoured the PATC buses.

The result of Chi-square test for the data in Table 4.15 reveals that the calculated value of χ^2 (1.86) is less than the table value. Therefore, the relationship between the age and passengers' preference is not significant.

3. Sex and Marital Status and Preference

As for the sex and marital status of the respondents, the

Exhibit 10
Passengers' Preference for PATC and Private Buses

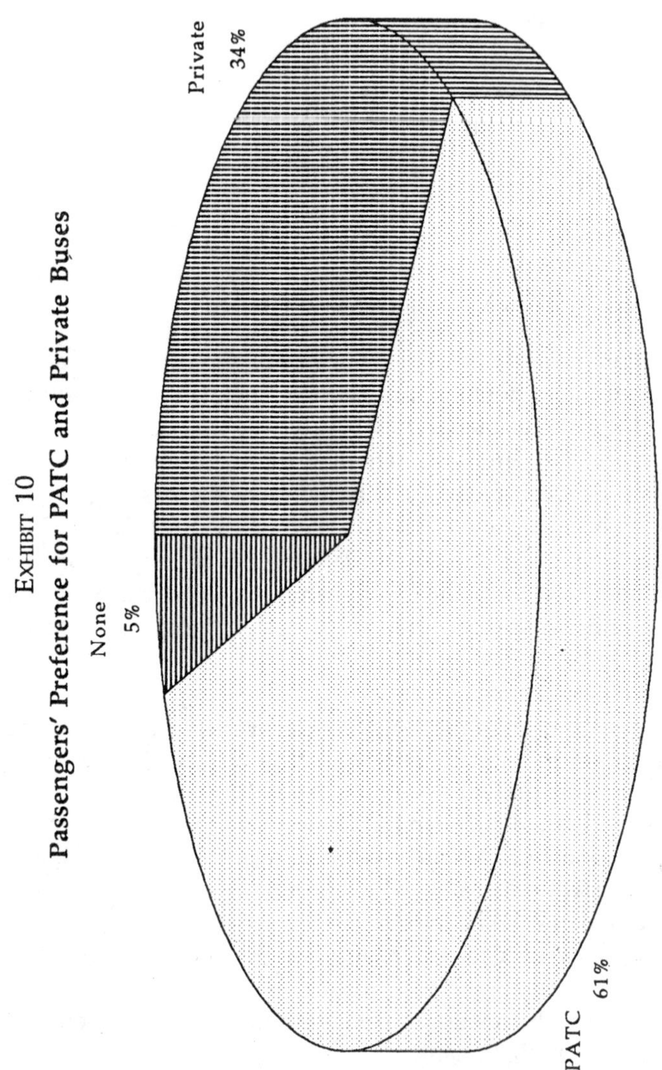

TABLE 4.15

Age and Passenger Preference of Bus

Age (years)	*No. of Respondents*		*Total*
	PATC	*Private*	
Less than 25 years	69(62)	42(38)	111
25-40	82 (66)	42(34)	124
40-55	28(70)	12(30)	40
Above 55	5(50)	5(50)	10
Total	184(65)	101(35)	285

Calculated χ^2=1.86 P=0.603
Table χ^2 = 7.82 Not Significant

TABLE 4.16

Sex and Passenger Preference of Bus

Sex	*No. of Respondents*		*Total*
	PATC	*Private*	
Male	135 (65)	72(35)	207
Female	49(63)	29(37)	78
Total	184(65)	101(35)	285

Calculated χ^2 =0.0567 P=0.8117
Table χ^2 = 3.84 Not Significant

majority of the male as well as female, married and unmarried respondents have preferred PATC buses. The percentage of such respondents to the total number of respondents is around 65 per cent in their respective categories.

The results of Chi-square test for the data in Tables 4.16 and 4.17 reveal that the calculated values of χ^2 are less than the table values. Therefore, the relationship between the sex as well as marital status and passengers' preference is not significant.

TABLE 4.17

Marital Status and Passenger Preference of Bus

Marital Status	*No. of Respondents*		*Total*
	PATC	*Private*	
Married	98(64)	55(36)	'53
Unmarried	86(65)	46(35)	132
Total	184 (65)	101(35)	285

Calculate χ^2 =0.0048 P=0.944

Table χ^2 =3.84 Not Significant

4. Level of Education and Preference

Education is yet another factor determines one's opinion on a particular aspect. The respondents have been grouped into six categories based on their level of education, starting from Illiterates of Post-Graduates/Professional.

It is quite interesting to note that as the level of education increases the preference for PATC buses too increases. The

TABLE 4.18

Level of Education and Passenger Preference of Bus

Education	*No. of Respondents*		*Total*
	PATC	*Private*	
Illiterates	2(33)	4(67)	6
Educated upto SSLC	16(53)	14(47)	30
Educated upto HSC	34(60)	23(40)	57
Diploma holders	27(66)	14(34)	41
Degree holders	59(69)	26(31)	85
PGs and Professionals	46(70)	20(30)	66
Total	184(65)	101(35)	285

Calculated χ^2=6.476 P=0.2625

Table χ^2=11.07 Not Significant

illiterates have more preference for private buses wherein 67 per cent of the respondents in that category have preferred private buses, whereas most of the highly educated respondents (P.G. and Professional degree holders) have preferred PATC buses, 70 per cent of such respondents having favoured PATC buses. The rest of the respondents' preference for PATC buses increases as the level of education increases.

The result of Chi-square test for the data in Table 4.18 reveals that the calculated value of χ^2 (6.476) is less than the table value. Therefore, the relationship between education and passengers' preference is not significant.

5. Occupation and Preference

In Table 4.19, the respondents have been divided into 6 categories on the basis of their occupation, viz., Employees in Government Sector (86), Employees in Private Sector (46), Executives in Private/Government Sector (35), Businessmen (36), Students (39) and Others (43), which include Agriculturists,

TABLE 4.19

Occupation and Passenger Preference of Bus

Occupation	*No. of Respondents*		*Total*
	PATC	*Private*	
1. Employees in Govt. sector	61(71)	25(29)	86
2. Employees in Private Sector	31(67)	15(33)	46
3. Executives in Private/ Govt. Sector	22(63)	21(37)	43
4. Business Men	24(67)	12(33)	36
5. Students	24(62)	15(38)	39
6. Others	22(51)	13(49)	35
Total	184(65)	101(35)	285

Calculate χ^2=5.33 P= 0.377
Table χ^2 =11.07 Not Significant

workers, Self-employed and Unemployed.

Among these categories, employees in Government Sector have largely preferred PATC buses, which account for 71 per cent and the least frequency occurred in the 'others' category where 22 respondents have preferred PATC, accounting for 51 per cent. The percentage of respondents who have preferred PATC buses among the rest of the categories is around 65 per cent. Thus the respondents in all the occupational groups prefer PATC buses to private buses, except the respondents in the 'other category' who prefer both PATC and private buses equally.

The result of Chi-square test for the data in Table 4.19, reveals that the calculated value of χ^2 (5.33) is less than the table value. Therefore, the relationship between the occupation and passengers' preference is not significant.

6. Level of Income and Preference

Table 4.20 reveals that the respondents in all the categories of income level favoured PATC buses. The percentage of respondents who favoured PATC buses is above 60 per cent. It is 62 per cent for respondents whose income is upto Rs. 1000, 65 per cent for the respondents with income ranging from Rs. 1001 to Rs. 3000 and 68 per cent for the respondents with monthly income of above Rs. 3000. It is inferred that passengers with lower income have relatively more preference for private

TABLE 4.20

Level of Income and Passenger Preference of Bus

Income (Rs.)	*No. of Respondents*		*Total*
	PATC	*Private*	
Upto 1000	45 (62)	28(38)	73
1001-3000	99(65)	54(35)	153
Above 3000	21(68)	10(32)	31
Total	165(64)	92(36)	257

Calculated χ^2=0.394 P=0.821

Table χ^2=5.99 Not Significant

buses than the respondents with the higher income.

The result of Chi-square test for the data in Table 4.20 reveals that the calculated value of X^2 (0.394) is less than the table value. Therefore, the relationship between the income and passengers' preference is not significant.

7. Purpose of Travel and Preference

The respondents were grouped into three categories on the basis of the purpose for which they mostly travel, viz., social, business and official. In all the groups, the respondents have preferred more of PATC buses than private buses. The percentage of respondents preferring PATC buses is 76 for those travelling for social purpose, 60 for those travelling for official purpose and 56 for business purpose.

The relatively less preference among business travellers for PATC may be attributed to the inflexible and cumbersome policy of PATC in allowing carrying luggage. The conductors of the buses too substantiate such inflexible policy of the corporation. So there is an urgent need to have a well-defined and flexible policy regarding allowing carrying luggage in PATC buses.

The result of Chi-square test for the data in Table 4.21, reveals that the calculated value of χ^2 (7.99) is more than the table value. Therefore, the relationship between the purpose of travel and the passengers' preference is significant at 5% level.

TABLE 4.21

Purpose of Travel and Passenger Preference of Bus

Purpose of travel	*No. of Respondents*		*Total*
	PATC	*Private*	
Social	74(76)	24(24)	98
Business	23(56)	18(44)	41
Official	87(60)	59(40)	146
Total	184(65)	101(35)	285

Calculated χ^2 =7.996 P=0.02

Table χ^2 =5.99 Significant at 5% level

8. Distance Travelled and Preference

When the passengers travel more, they gain more experience with the buses in which they travel. According to their experience they choose the bus.

TABLE 4.22

Distance Travelled and Passenger Preference of Bus

Distance Travelled per month in (kms)	*No. of Respondents*		*Total*
	PATC	*Private*	
Upto 500	99(67)	49(33)	148
501-1000	40(68)	19(32)	59
Above 1000	45(58)	33(42)	78
Total	184(65)	101(35)	285

Calculated χ^2 =2.23 P=0.33
Table χ^2=5.99 Not Significant

It has been observed from Table 4.22 that all the group of respondents, irrespective of the distance travelled, they have preferred PATC buses more than the private buses.

The result of Chi-square test for the data in Table 4.22 reveals that the calculated value of χ^2 (2.33) is less than the table value. Therefore, the relationship between distance travelled and passengers' preference is not significant.

9. Frequency of Travel and Preference

Frequency of travel by the respondents is another criterion prompting the passengers to choose the bus. The respondents have been grouped as Daily Travellers (130), Frequent Travellers (81) and Occasional Travellers (74) as shown in Table 4.23.

In all the groups PATC buses are more preferred than private buses. It is also observed that as the frequency of travel decreases the preference for PATC increases and preference for private buses decreases. The more frequency of travel and the decreasing trend for PATC may be attributed to the fact that the private bus operators try to attract the more frequent travellers

TABLE 4.23

Frequency of Travel and the Passenger Preference of Bus

Frequency of Travel	*No. of Respondents*		*Total*
	PATC	*Private*	
Daily	70(54)	60(46)	130
Frequently	57(70)	24(30)	81
Occasionally	57(77)	17(23)	74
Total	184(64)	101(360)	285

Calculate χ^2 =12.74 P=0.001
Table χ^2 =5.99 Significant at .1% level

by giving concessions in fares and allowing them to carry luggage at low charges. The state-owned PATC may not be able to offer such concessions due to their rules and regulations and impersonal administration.

The result of Chi-square test for the data in Table 4.23 reveals that the calculated value of χ^2 (12.74) is more than the table value. Therefore, the relationship between the frequency of travel and passengers' preference is significant at .1% level.

10. Possession of Personal Vehicle and Preference

It is difficult to attract passengers who own personal vehicles, since the expectation of those passengers would be generally higher than those who do not own one.

Table 4.24 reveals that all the group of the respondents preferred PATC buses more than private buses. The percentage of respondents preferring PATC buses is the highest for respondents owning moped and the lowest for those not owning any vehicle.

The result of Chi-square test for the data in Table 4.24 reveals that the calculated value of χ^2 (2.11) is less than the table value. Therefore, the relationship between the owning of vehicles and the passengers' preference is not significant.

TABLE 4.24

Possession of Personal Vehicle and Passenger Preference of Bus

Type of Vehicle	*No. of Respondents*		*Total*
	PATC	*Private*	
None	128(62)	78(38)	206
Moped	20(74)	7(26)	27
Motor Cycle/Scooter	32(70)	14(30)	46
Car	4(67)	2(33)	6
Total	184(65)	101(35)	285

Calculated χ^2=2.112 P=0.549
Table χ^2=7.82 Not Significant

6. REASONS FOR PREFERENCE OF PATC/PRIVATE BUSES

The discussions made so far in this chapter relate to the study of bus usage and preference by the sample passenger respondents. In this section, an attempt is made to identify the reasons for their preference towards PATC or private buses separately.

Nine reasons were stated in the interview schedule. Each respondent was asked to rank any five reasons according to their choice. Weights from 5 to 1 were allotted in the order of 1st Rank to 5th Rank and weighted score for each reason was arrived at, and for easy comparison, the average weighted scores per respondent were also calculated. Then all the reasons were ranked in the order of the weighted scores that each reasons acquired.

1. Reasons for Preferring PATC Buses

The reasons for preferring PATC buses by the respondents with the respective weighted scores as given by them and their order among the stated reasons are given in Table 4.25.

It has been observed from Table 4.24 that 'Quick Service' was accorded the first rank as the reason for preferring PATC buses, with the highest score of 718, the average weighted score being 3.9 per respondent. There is a vast difference of 213 scores between the scores accorded to the first reason and the second foremost reason. The second foremost reason namely, 'Availability of bus during the convenient time and place' has been awarded with the weighted score of 505 (Average weighted score—2.74 per respondent). The next rank falls on two reasons with a weighted score of 359 each and consequently 3.5 rank was allotted to both the reasons viz., 'Maintenance and appearance of the bus' and 'Safety and Reliability'. The average weighted score for both the reasons were 1.95 each. The fifth rank was awarded to the reason 'Not satisfied with the private bus operations' with a weighted score of 244 (average score 1.17). 'Cooperative attitude of Crew members' has gained the weighted score of 216, with an average score of 1.17 and emerged as the 6th reason for preferring PATC buses. The rest of the reasons for the passengers' preference, are 'Concessional facilities', 'Easy to carry luggage' (98), and 'other reasons' (94), whose average scores are less than one, ranging between 0.5 and 0.6. The respondents are not satisfied with the operation of private buses due to overloading, stopping at unauthorised places, rash driving, playing tape recorders and patronage to government bus transport undertakings.

Thus the most popular advantage of PATC is the offering of 'Quick Service' and the 'Availability of service at convenient place and time' comes next. The third motivating factor consists of three reasons, for which the respondents have given almost equal weight. They are 'Maintenance and Appearance of the bus', 'Safety and Reliability' and 'Cooperative attitude of Crew members'. The rest of the reasons stated are not strong enough to attract the passengers to PATC buses, as the scores gained by such reasons are negligible.

2. Reasons for Preferring Private Bus

The motivating factors that prompt the passengers for preferring Private bus operations and their order have been exhibited in Table 4.25.

It is quite interesting to note that in the case of private bus operators also, respondents have stated 'Quick Service' as the foremost reason for preferring private buses. The weighted score

TABLE 4.25

Reasons for Preference of PATC/Private Buses

Sl. No.	*Reasons*	*PATC*		*Private*	
		Weighted Score	*Rank*	*Weighted Score*	*Rank*
(i)	Quick Service	718 (3.90)	1	278 (2.75)	1
(ii)	Availability during convenient hour and place	505 (2.74)	2	196 (1.94)	4
(iii)	Maintenance and appearance of the bus	359 (1.95)	3.5	202 (2.0)	3
(iv)	Safety and reliability	359 (1.95)	3.5	117 (1.16)	7
(v)	Not satisfied with the operation of other Bus	244 (1.32)	5	34 (0.34)	9
(vi)	Cooperative attitude of Crew members	216 (1.17)	6	191 (1.89)	6
(vii)	Concessional facilities	118 (0.64)	7	195 (1.93)	5
(viii)	Easy to carry luggage	98 (0.53)	8	214 (2.12)	2
(ix)	Any other Reason	94 (0.51)	9	50 (0.5)	8

Note: Figures in brackets are Mean Scores.

for this is 278 and the average score is 2.75. However, the average score is less than that of PATC (3.9). The second rank has been accorded to 'Easy to carry luggage', with a weighted score of 214 and the average score of 2.11. 'Maintenance and appearance', 'Availability during convenient hour and time', 'Concessional facilities' ar.d 'Cooperative attitude of Crew members' have been ranked next. The seventh rank has gone to 'Safety and reliability' with a weighted score of 117. The last two ranks (8th and 9th) have been given to 'Other reasons' and 'Not satisfied with the operation of PATC' whose weighted score is negligible and the average score is less than 0.5 in both the cases.

It is inferred that the most popular advantage of private operators is the offering of 'Quick service' and 'Ease in carrying luggage' and the second in order is good maintenance of vehicles, offering personalised service and concessional facilities. Concessions are extended in the form of reduced fares to regular passengers, concessional fare to group travellers and free travel for children.

3. Reason for Preferring PATC/Private Buses—Comparison

In Tamil Nadu, there has been a happy mixture of both Private and Public Sectors in transport operations. In order to identify the special features of bus operations by Private and Public Sector against each other, a comparison of reasons, state by the respondents for preferring a certain type of bus operation is made. A close look at the reasons show that two reasons viz., 'Quick Service' and 'Cooperative attitude of Crew members', have been given the same rank for both PATC as well as Private buses. However, there has been difference in the average scores between PATC and Private operations for both the reasons. With regard to 'Wuick Service' the average score of PATC buses has been 3.9 and that of the private buses has been 2.75, showing a vast difference of 1.15 score, but in the case of the latter reason, 'Crew Members are cooperative', the average score for PATC (1.17) is less than that of Private buses (1.89). So it is observed that though the respondents have given the same rank order for the above two reasons—'Quick Service' is found more in the case of PATC buses and 'Crew members are cooperative' in the case of private buses than PATC buses. The maximum difference in rank order of PATC and private buses is found in the case of 'Carrying Luggage'.

It is inferred that both Private and PATC operations are giving their utmost service to the public. The private operators are small operators and ply buses mostly as shuttle services between town and also between villages within a short distance. They are able to give more personalised service to travellers, whereas the Government owned PATC, being a big operator operating mostly on long-routes and working under corporate culture is above to give relatively quick and efficient service to the passengers.

7. SUMMARY

The opinion survey of the respondents as to their bus usage profile, preference for buses between private operators and state owned PATC and reasons for such preference have been undertaken in this chapter.

The study reveals that passengers used to travel mostly by PATC buses which is closely followed by private buses and third comes the other government corporation buses. This is in tune with the number of fleets held by each operator. However, it is interesting to note that certain group of passengers such as 'low income group of respondents', passengers who travel for 'Business purposes', and passengers who 'travel more distance' have used the buses of both private and PATC equally. The 'illiterate' and 'aged' passengers have used more of private buses than PATC buses. In all the factor groups the buses of other corporations have been used the least by the respondents.

With regard to the preference between PATC and Private buses, it has been observed that majority of the passengers have preferred PATC buses to private buses, except in the case of illiterate respondents who have preferred private buses more than PATC buses. However, the respondents' level of preference for PATC varies among the different groups of passengers based on their socio-economic background.

The important reasons for preferring PATC buses have been 'Quick Service' followed by 'availability at convenient place and time'. For the private buses also the first reason has been the 'Quick Service' closely followed by 'easy to carry luggage'. From the reasons given by the respondents for their preference of PATC, it is inferred that they expect quick and efficient service from PATC buses, whereas in the case of private buses it is the personalised service that passengers expect.

5

Passengers' Satisfaction with their Travel—Comparison of PATC and Private Buses

1. INTRODUCTION

In this chapter, an attempt is made to measure the extent of satisfaction of the passengers on the various aspects of their travel in the buses of the public sector transport corporation viz., PATC and in the private buses in North Arcot region.

The objective of any business is to satisfy the wants of the customers. There are two yardsticks to measure the success of any business. One is through quantitative factor such as profit, capital appreciation and increase in the value of assets. The other is through ascertaining the satisfaction of the customers regarding the products sold and services extended by the business unit. The second method is more appropriate in the case of public utility services such as transport. Bus transport service is used by all sections if the people such as businessmen, farmers, middle class, salary earners, housewives, students and industrial workers. The opinion of the different groups of passengers vary according to their experiences, perceptions, family and societal background. Therefore, ascertaining the opinion of all groups of passengers is imperative. One method of ascertaining such opinion is to measure the extent or level of satisfaction of the individual passengers on the various aspects of their travel.

Passenger transport service is extended by many bus operators belonging to both public and private sectors in Tamil Nadu. STUs operate a major bulk of the bus services. Private operators also ply buses. Co-existence of both the public and private sector in this public utility service leads to competition between the two. The policy of the Tamil Nadu Government relating to the role of the private sector in running passenger transport has been one of allowing limited competition. Ever since the formation of the State Transport Undertakings in the year 1971, private sector has been allowed to operate only to a limited extent. The present policy of the government is that a single private bus operator can run only upto 5 vehicles. However, this ceiling on individual bus operators has in no way restricted the extent of competition between the public and private sectors. This trend of severe competition between private bus operators and Government Road Transport Corporations is reflected very much in certain routes as many private operators run their buses in the same route along with government corporation buses. The extent of such competition is generally more in mofussil routes.

The passengers have opportunity to travel in the buses operated by both private operators and government corporations. Therefore, comparative evaluation of passenger transport service extended by private operators and government corporation buses should be made. Such a comparative evaluation is expected to reveal the extent of satisfaction derived by the passengers in both the buses and also the areas for improvement in the bus services operated by both private sector and government sector.

2. PASSENGER SATISFACTION

Satisfaction of the passengers on the various aspects of their travel is abstract and qualitative. It cannot be measured directly. It can be measured only indirectly through their opinions or responses to various aspects of their travel. A scale by name "Passenger Satisfaction Scale" has been constructed to measure the level of satisfaction of each passenger respondent. The scale is a Likert type-five points scale containing 40 items relating to the various aspects of travel. These 40 items have been grouped under five heads as given below, with the number of items under each head in brackets.

1. Passenger Comforts (10)
2. Punctuality and Regularity (10)
3. Safety and Reliability (6)
4. Crew Related Satisfaction (6)
5. Social Responsibility (8).

The responses of the respondents to the items have been recorded on five degrees on satisfaction. The most desired response is awarded four scores and the least zero. Thus the Passenger Satisfaction Scale has maximum score of 160 (40×4). The respondents have been grouped into three, based on their level of satisfaction as (1) Low, (2) Medium, and (3) High. Passengers with less than 25 per cent of the total scores (0 to 40 scores) have been grouped into 'Low Satisfaction' category, passengers with total score between 26 and 75 per cent (41 to 120 scores) under 'Medium Satisfaction' category and the respondent with above 75 (above 121 scores) per cent of the total scores in the 'High Satisfaction' category.

3. EXTENT OF PASSENGER SATISFACTION IN PATC AND PRIVATE BUSES

The passenger satisfaction scores of the respondents range from 44 to 158 (Table 5.1) for PATC bus operation and their average satisfaction score is 99.61. Out of 300 respondents, 148 respondents have their respective satisfaction scores above the average and 152 respondents below the average. As the average passenger satisfaction score is 99.61 out of the maximum of 160, it can be inferred that the Passenger Satisfaction with regard to PATC bus operation among the commuters in the North Arcot Region is satisfactory.

It has been observed that the Passenger Satisfaction Scores of the sample respondents in private buses is 97.85 and the individual scores range from 2 to 154. The number of respondents

TABLE 5.1

Variation in Passenger Satisfaction of the Respondents Between PATC and Private Buses

Bus operation	*Average Satisfaction Score*	*Range*	*No. of Respondents*	
			Above ASS	*Below ASS*
PATC	99.61	44 to 158	148	152
Private	97.85	02 to 154	168	132

above the average satisfaction score were 168 and 132 respondents were below the average satisfaction score. As the average PSS is 97.85 out of the total score of 160, it is inferred that commuters are satisfied with regard to private bus operations too. However, as the mean satisfaction score is higher for PATC buses than that for private buses it can be inferred that the respondents are relatively more satisfied with their travel in PATC buses than in private buses.

The respondents were classified into three groups (Table 5.2) viz., 1. Low Satisfied, 2. Medium Satisfied, and 3. High Satisfied on the basis of their individual Passenger Satisfaction Scores.

In the case of PATC buses, out of 300 respondents, none falls in the category of 'Low Satisfaction'. There are 255 respondents representing 85 per cent in the 'Medium Satisfaction' group and 45 respondents representing 15 per cent in the 'High Satisfaction' group.

With regard to private buses, out of 300 respondents, 5 respondents representing less than 2 per cent have 'Low Satisfaction', 248 respondents are in 'Medium Satisfaction' group constituting 82 per cent and 47 respondents representing 16 per cent of the sample, are in 'High Satisfaction' group.

It is inferred that the passengers are satisfied with both the operation of PATC buses as well as Private buses. However, the passengers' satisfaction with the operation of PATC is marginally higher than that of private bus operation.

The Paired 't' Test has been applied to ascertain the

TABLE 5.2

Extent of Passenger Satisfaction of the Respondents

Level of Satisfaction	*PATC*	*Private*
Low	Nil	05 (02)
Medium	255 (85)	248 (82)
High	45 (15)	47 (16)
Total	300	300

significance of the difference in the average satisfaction scores between PATC and private buses. The test reveals that the difference is not significant (Table 5.3). Hence, the hypothesis that the passengers are more satisfied with their travel in PATC buses than in private buses.

4. PASSENGERS' SATISFACTION AND OPERATIONAL ASPECTS OF BUS OPERATIONS

Satisfaction of the passengers with their travel arises from the extent of satisfaction they get from various aspects of their travel. Therefore, the Passenger Satisfaction Scale constructed in this study consists of items relating to 40 aspects of travel. These 40 items have been grouped under five heads and the relevant

TABLE 5.3

Difference in Passenger Satisfaction Between PATC and Private Buses : Paired 't' Test

No. of Respondents	*Difference*		*'t' Value*	*Significance*
	Mean	*SD*		
300	1.7	28.00	1.05	NS

questions related to each head have been given under the heads, as shown on pages 118 and 119.

The extent of overall passenger satisfaction derived by a passenger depends on the extent of satisfaction derived by him from the various aspects of his travel under these heads. Hence the extent of the respondents' satisfaction with the various aspects has been attempted in this section. And a comparison has been made between PATC and private buses so as to identify the strong and weak areas in relation to each other.

Table 5.4 and 5.5 exhibit the extent of passenger satisfaction on various components in travelling in PATC and private buses respectively.

TABLE 5.4

Components of Passenger Satisfaction in Travelling in PATC Buses

Sl. No.	*Components*	*Average Satis-faction score*	*Range*	*No. of Respondents*		*SD*
				Above ASS	*Below ASS*	
1.	Passenger comforts	25.85	7 to 40	165	135	6.03
2.	Punctuality and Regularity	24.21	3 to 40	151	149	6.73
3.	Safety and Reliability	15.54	0 to 24	158	142	3.91
4.	Crew Related Satisfaction	14.86	0 to 24	169	131	4.39
5.	Social Responsibility	19.15	5 to 32	146	154	5.03
6.	Overall Passenger Satisfaction	99.61	44 to 158	148	152	20.80

1. Passenger Comforts

Any passenger, young or old, male or female, educated or uneducated, would expect the bus operators to provide a comfortable travel. Good seating arrangements, proper ventilation, sufficient space inside the bus, proper lighting, cleanliness and ease in boarding and alighting are the aspects that may provide comforts to the passengers which, in turn, may enhance the level of satisfaction. An attempt has been made

TABLE 5.5

Components of Passenger Satisfaction in Travelling in Private Buses

Sl. No.	Components	Average Satis-faction score	Range	No. of Respondents		SD
				Above ASS	Below ASS	
1.	Passenger Comforts	27.08	0 to 40	167	133	7.59
2.	Punctuality and Regularity	23.42	0 to 40	160	140	7.36
3.	Safety and Reliability	13.62	0 to 24	167	133	4.74
4.	Crew Related Satisfaction	14.30	0 to 24	167	133	4.60
5.	Social Responsibility	19.43	0 to 32	147	153	5.24
6.	Overall Passenger Satisfaction	97.85	0 to 154	168	132	23.88

in this part to study the level of satisfaction as to this component.

It is observed from Table 5.4 that the average satisfaction score of the respondents as to the 'Passenger Comforts' in PATC buses is 25.85 (65 per cent) against the total score of 40. The number of respondents above and below the average satisfaction score are 165 and 135 respectively. The average satisfaction score of sample respondents for private buses (Table 5.5) is 27.08 (68 per cent) which is marginally higher than that of PATC buses and the number of respondents above and below the average satisfaction score are 167 and 133. It is inferred that the passengers are relatively more satisfied with regard to Passenger Comforts in private buses than in PATC buses. This is inspite of the fact that PATC mostly plays the lead role in introducing new buses by replacing the buses after 6 years of operation or 7 lakh kms run, whichever is earlier. The lower satisfaction in this component for PATC buses may be attributed, to some extent, to the poor maintenance of buses, including uncleanliness, non-replacement of broken or worn-out parts and unattended minor repairs, whereas the private bus operators give more attention to these aspects.

EXHIBIT 11

Components of Passenger Satisfation in PATC/Private Buses

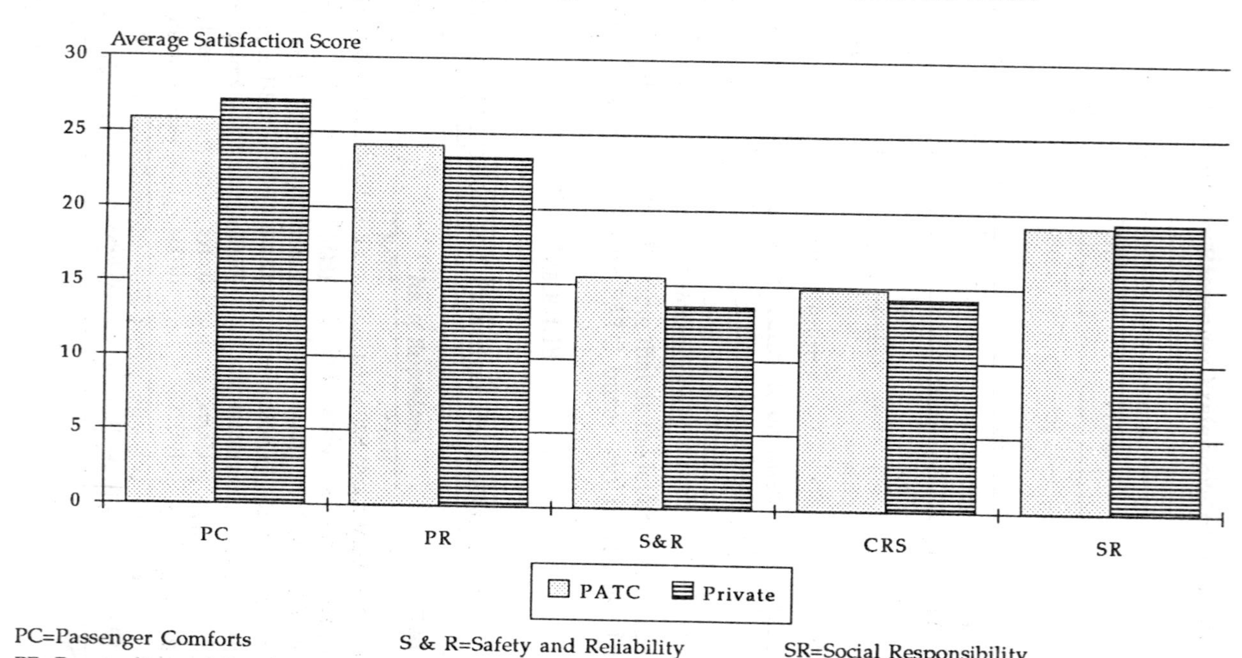

PC=Passenger Comforts
PR=Punctuality and Regularity
S & R=Safety and Reliability
CRS=Crew Related Satisfaction
SR=Social Responsibility

2. Punctuality and Regularity

Punctuality and regularity is another criterion for the efficient operation of buses. If the operator does not follow punctuality, it may cause great hardship to the commuters—not only that they may go to their office and other place of work late, but at times some of them may also miss the changeover bus/train, which further delays their travel. Regularity must also be adhered to, in the sense that there should be no cancellation of any service/trip, which may disappoint the commuters. An attempt has been made to study the opinion of the sample respondents with regard to punctuality and Regularity.

It has been observed (Tables 5.4 and 5.5) that the average Passenger Satisfaction Score for Punctuality and Regularity of bus services has been 24.21 (61 per cent) for PATC operations and 23.42 (59 per cent) for private bus operations out of the total score of 40. The number of respondents above and below the average satisfaction score has been respectively 151 and 149 for PATC buses and 160 and 140 for private buses. It is inferred that the passengers are satisfied with the Punctuality and Reliability of both the operators, viz., PATC and private. However, comparison of PATC and private operators in this regard reveals that the passengers' satisfaction is relatively more for PATC buses than for private buses.

3. Safety and Reliability

No accidents, negligible break-downs and consistency of speed are some of the aspects that the commuters would expect from any bus operator, irrespective of the respondent's age, sex, education and income. The related questions of this nature were posed to the sample respondents under the heading 'Safety and Reliability' and their opinion were sought as to their satisfaction with these aspects in PATC and private buses.

It has been noted (Tables 5.4 and 5.5) that PATC buses have been placed in the high order, where the average passenger satisfaction score is 15.54 (65 per cent) out of the total score of 24 and the average score for private buses is 13.62 (57 per cent). The number of respondents above and below the average score has been 158 and 142 for PATC buses and 167 and 133 for private buses respectively. It is inferred that the level of satisfaction as to 'Safety and Reliability' has been higher in PATC buses than in private buses. The reason for this phenomenon may be that the PATC drivers are well-trained and work for limited hours in a day. Apart from this, PATC buses maintain consistency in speed, whereas the private buses stop at many unauthorised stops, thereby wasting time and afterwards run at a greater speed to cover the distance within the stipulated time, which may, in turn, lead to accidents.

4. Crew Related Satisfaction

Crew members are the persons who have significant role to play in determining the passengers' satisfaction. They are the persons who have direct contact with the passengers of different background and needs. Courteous behaviour and helpful attitude of the crew is expected to enhance the level of satisfaction of the commuters. Crew-related satisfaction of the sample respondents has been given in Tables 5.4 and 5.5, which exhibit that the passengers' average satisfaction scores have been 14.86 (62 per cent) against the total score of 24 for PATC buses and 14.3 (60 per cent) for private buses. The number of passengers above and below the average satisfaction score has been 169 and 131 respectively for PATC buses and 167 and 133 respondents in the case of private buses. Thus, it is inferred that the attitude of the passengers towards the crew has been almost the same both in the case of PATC buses as well as in the case of private buses. Difference in ownership has not contributed to difference in crew-related satisfaction.

5. Social Responsibility

Business organisations are not only economic institutions but also a social systems and the products and consequences of business are inevitably social in a far broader sense than being economic. This philosophy equally applies to the business of bus operation too. Social obligations that the bus operator may undertake include concession to specific categories of less privileged passengers, such as the handicapped, the aged and students, plying buses in uneconomic routes and operating services during the lean period, late night and early morning hours.

The attitude of the sample respondents as to the existence of these factors in the operations of buses by PATC and private operation has been studied. It has been observed (Table 5.4 and 5.5) that the average satisfaction score is 19.15 (60 per cent) for PATC against the total score of 32 and for the private buses it is 19.43 (61 per cent). The number of respondents whose satisfaction scores are above the average satisfaction score are 146 and below the average satisfaction score are 154 for PATC and the respective figures for private buses are 147 and 153.

It is inferred that the respondents are satisfied with regard to the social obligations rendered by both the operators. However, the respondents are marginally more satisfied with the operation of private buses in this regard than with the PATC buses, which is supposed to cater to the needs of the society in a bigger way than the private operators. Being a big operator, PATC is better placed in discharging social responsibility than the private bus operators. However, at times, the organisation's rules and regulations make the PATC unable to reach the needy people. For instance, PATC allow free travel for blind persons from the place of their residence to the place of work. This concession is allowed only in town route services. Moreover, such persons should get prior permission from the Head Office/ Branch Office and the concession is being given only between fixed points (place) for a fixed period and the points (place) of travel cannot be changed within the period. But in reality, a self-employed blindman, for example, may get work from different places and as a result of the above said rule, he cannot travel free to the places other than that mentioned in the concession pass issued to him. Thus he is unable to make use of the free travel facilities whereas in the case of private buses, he can avail himself of the concession/free travel facilities with less formalities, at times, the conductor of the bus himself uses his discretion and allows such concessions.

5. PASSENGER SATISFACTION INDEX

Passenger satisfaction is the key to successful traffic management. In the above analysis, the overall passenger satisfaction of the respondents as well as their satisfaction as to the different components such as comfort, punctuality and regularity, safety and reliability, crew related satisfaction and social responsibility have been studied for both PATC and private bus operation and comparison has been made thereto. In order to arrive at a single figure which may depict the level of passenger satisfaction for easy comparison, Passenger Satisfaction Index (PSI) has been designed for the two sectors on the line of Quality Service Index (QSI) as developed by Dr. P.G. Patankar.[1]

PSI is a weighted Index computed by assigning appropriate weights for different service factors. As safety and reliability is the most important aspect that a passenger would expect from a bus operator than any other comfort or facility, the maximum weight of 30 is assigned to it; it is followed by punctuality and regularity for which 20 weights have been assigned. The rest of the components viz., passenger comfort, crew-related satisfaction and social responsibility have been given equal weights of 10 each. Thus it has been attempted to arrive at a single figure of PSI by multiplying the average of the scores awarded to all the respondents for the different questions under the components by the respective weight assigned to the component. This process is depicted in the formula given below:

$$PSI = \frac{AW_1 + BW_2 + CW_3 + DW_4 + EW_5}{W_1 + W_2 + W_3 + W_4 + W_5}$$

where,

A = Average Satisfaction Score for Passenger Comforts,
B = Average Satisfaction Score for Punctuality and Regularity,
C = Average Satisfaction Score for Safety and Reliability,
D = Average Satisfaction Score for Crew-Related Satisfaction,
E = Average Satisfaction Score for Social Responsibility,
W_1 = Weight assigned to Passenger Comfort = 10,
W_2 = Weight assigned to Punctuality and Regularity = 20,
W_3 = Weight assigned to Safety and Reliability = 30,
W_4 = Weight assigned to Crew-Related Satisfaction = 10,
W_5 = Weight assigned to Social Responsibility =10.

The PSI, thus computed has been 19.36 for PATC and 18.56 for private buses. It is inferred from this that passengers are relatively more satisfied with PATC buses than with private buses in North Arcot Region.

6. FACTORS INFLUENCING PASSENGERS' SATISFACTION

This part of analysis aims at relating the passengers' satisfaction with their social and economic factors such as place of residence, age, sex, marital status, income, education, occupation, purpose of travel, distance travelled, frequency of travel and owning personal vehicle.

1. Place of Residence and Passenger Satisfaction

People in urban areas enjoy more comforts and facilities than those in rural areas. Generally, the urban commuter population consists of middle class salary earners and manual workers. Their standard of living is higher than the rural commuters consisting of agricultural workers, housewives and petty traders. Therefore, the expectation of the urban commuters relating to the various travel criteria is generally higher than that of the rural commuters and hence it is expected that urban commuters would be less satisfied than the rural commuters.

Out of 300 respondents, 171 (57 per cent) respondents were from Urban areas. The average satisfaction score of the Urban respondents is 98.6 for PATC bus and there were 86 respondents above the average satisfaction score and 85 respondents below the average satisfaction score (Table 5.6). Their average satisfaction score for private buses is 94.5 and the number of respondents above and below the average satisfaction score were 75 and 96. It is observed from the above figures that the Urban passengers are more satisfied with PATC buses than with private buses.

There were 129 rural respondents among the sample. Their average satisfaction score for PATC bus operation was 101 and there were 67 respondents above and 62 respondents below the average satisfaction score. With regard to the private buses, their average satisfaction score is 102.34, which is marginally

TABLE 5.6

Relationship between Place of Residence and Passenger Satisfaction

Place of Residence	*No. of respondents*	*Satisfaction Scores*			
		PATC		*Private*	
		Mean	*S.D.*	*Mean*	*S.D.*
Urban	171	98.6	21.2	94.5	24.77
Rural	129	101.0	20.22	102.34	21.95
Total	300	99.6	20.8	97.9	23.88

TABLE 5.7

Place of Residence and Passenger Satisfaction between PATC and Private Buses : Paired 't' Test

Place of Residence	*Difference*		*'t' Value*	*Significance*
	Mean	*S.D.*		
Urban	3.9942	27.98	1.87	NS
Rural	-1.3411	27.83	0.55	NS

higher than that of PATC buses. There were 62 respondents above and 67 respondents below the average satisfaction score. It has been observed that the rural passengers are marginally less satisfied with the operation of PATC buses than that of private buses. This is contrary to the hypothesis that rural passengers are more satisfied with PATC buses than with private buses. This may be due to the concessions extended to the regular passengers by the conductors of private buses, allowing the rural passengers to carry luggage and offering other personal services.

Paired 't' test applied to ascertain the significance of the difference in the average satisfaction scores between PATC and private buses has revealed that the differences in the average passenger satisfaction scores are not significant for both Urban and Rural passengers (Table 5.7). Therefore, the hypothesis formulated in this connection that Urban passengers are more satisfied with their travel in PATC buses than in private buses is rejected.

2. Age and Passenger Satisfaction

The travel need and the demand of the passengers may differ according to the mental attitude and maturity of the passengers. Age contributes to the level of maturity and hence there may be differences in passenger satisfaction due to age difference. The respondents have been grouped into three categories viz., 1. Young (upto 30 years), 2. Middle Aged (between 31 and 50 years), and 3. Old (above 50 years).

TABLE 5.8

Relationship between Age and Passenger Satisfaction

Age Group	*No. of respondents*	*Satisfaction Scores*			
		PATC		*Private*	
		Mean	*S.D.*	*Mean*	*S.D.*
Young	167	99.01	19.80	97.88	24.80
Middle	110	100.15	21.14	98.21	23.60
Old	23	101.00	26.18	101.13	18.40
Total	300	99.6	20.8	97.9	23.88

The average satisfaction score of the 167 young respondents with regard to PATC operation was 99 and there were 86 respondents above the mean satisfaction score and 81 respondents below the mean satisfaction score. There were 110 middle aged passengers. Their average satisfaction score was 100.15 and there were 55 respondents above as well as below the average satisfaction score. The average satisfaction score was 101 for the 23 old respondents and it has been noted that 12 respondents were above and 11 respondents were below the average satisfaction score. It has been observed from the above discussion that the aged respondents are more satisfied with the operation of buses by PATC, followed by the middle aged and young respondents. The average satisfaction score increases when age increases.

With regard to private buses, the average satisfaction score of the young respondents was 97.88 and that of the middle aged was 98.21. The aged respondents' mean satisfaction score was 101.13 and there were 11 respondents above and 12 respondents below the mean satisfaction score. The number of respondents above and below the average satisfaction score among the young respondents were 81 and 86 and among the middle aged respondents were 44 and 66.

It is inferred that the aged passengers are equally satisfied with both PATC and private buses. Whereas, the middle aged and young respondents are more satisfied with PATC buses than with private buses.

Table 5.9 reveals that the difference in the average passenger satisfaction scores between PATC and private buses are not significant for all the three age groups of respondents. Hence, the hypothesis that the young passengers are more satisfied with their travel in PATC buses than in private buses is rejected.

3. Sex and Passenger Satisfaction

The expectation of the female passengers, with regard to travel comforts and other aspects of bus operations may be more than that of male respondents, who may manage certain travel difficulties and discomforts. An attempt has been made to

TABLE 5.9

Age and Passenger Satisfaction between PATC and Private Buses : Paired 't' Test

Age Group	*Difference*		*'t'*	*Significance*
	Mean	*S.D.*	*Value*	
Young	1.7964	26.05	0.89	NS
Middle	1.9364	30.67	0.66	NS
Old	-0.1304	29.46	0.02	NS

study the relationship between the level of passenger satisfaction and sex.

TABLE 5.10

Relationship Between Sex and Passenger Satisfaction

Sex	*No. of respondents*	*Satisfaction Scores*			
		PATC		*Private*	
		Mean	*S.D.*	*Mean*	*S.D.*
Male	216	100.04	21.19	100.30	23.86
Female	84	98.40	19.72	91.60	22.90
Total	300	99.6	20.8	97.9	23.88

It has been observed from Table 5.10 that male respondents' are more satisfied than female respondents with both private and PATC buses. However, the difference is very marginal for male respondents and very much for the female.

TABLE 5.11

Sex and Passenger Satisfaction between PATC and Private Buses: Paired 't' Test

Sex	*Difference*		*'t' Value*	*Significance*
	Mean	*S.D.*		
Male	-0.2870	28.24	0.15	NS
Female	6.8095	26.84	2.32	5 % level

Table 5.11 reveals that the difference in the average passenger satisfaction scores between PATC and private buses is not significant for male respondents. The same is significant for the female respondents. Therefore, the hypothesis that the female passengers are more satisfied with their travel in PATC buses than in private buses is accepted.

4. Marital Status and Passenger Satisfaction

In Table 5.12 respondents have been grouped according to their marital status. The average satisfaction score of the married respondents is 99.57 for PATC and 99.65 for private buses and the number of respondents above and below the average satisfaction scores were 85 and 81 for PATC and the respective number of respondents for private bus operations were 75 and 91. The average satisfaction score of unmarried respondents for PATC was 99.59, which is higher than that of private bus operation, which was 95.69. The number of respondents above and below the average satisfaction score has been 67 each for PATC and for the private buses it has been 64 and 70.

TABLE 5.12

Relationship Between Marital Status and Passenger Satisfaction

Marital Status	*No. of respondents*	*Satisfaction Scores*			
		PATC		*Private*	
		Mean	*S.D.*	*Mean*	*S.D.*
Married	166	99.57	21.4	99.65	22.63
Unmarried	134	99.59	20.05	95.69	25.25
Total	300	99.6	20.8	97.9	23.88

It is inferred that the satisfaction level of the married respondents was the same for private as well as PATC buses whereas, the level of passenger satisfaction of the unmarried respondents was higher for PATC buses than for private buses.

Table 5.13 reveals that the differences in the average passenger satisfaction scores between PATC and private buses for both the married and unmarried groups are not significant. Hence, the hypothesis that unmarried passengers are more satisfied with their travel in PATC buses than in private buses is rejected.

5. Education and Passenger Satisfaction

The level of education one has, influences his capacity to

TABLE 5.13

Marital Status and Passenger Satisfaction Between PATC and Private Buses : Paired 't' Test

Marital Status	*Difference*		*'t'*	*Significance*
	Mean	*S.D.*	*Value*	
Married	-0.0783	28.41	0.04	NS
Unmarried	3.9030	27.42	1.65	NS

think objectively and the level of maturity. It is expected that a person with higher formal education will be more objective about the various aspects of passenger satisfaction such as comforts, safety and punctuality than the others.

The Passenger Satisfaction of the respondent has been studied with regard to their educational level, viz.,

1. Primary Education: The respondents who have studied upto 5th standard have been included under this group. There were 41 such respondents.

2. Secondary Education: The respondents who have studied upto 12th standard have been included in this group. There were 105 such respondents.

3. College Education: 154 respondents who have studied beyond 12th standard have been included in this group.

It has been observed from Table 5.14 that in both PATC and private buses, the respondents with 'Primary Education' have been relatively more satisfied than the other categories of respondents and their average satisfaction score for PATC is 105.76. The number of respondents above and below the average satisfaction score is 39 and 2. The average satisfaction score for private buses is 107.37, which is marginally higher than that of PATC buses.

The average satisfaction score of respondents with Secondary Education for PATC has been 100.59, which is relatively higher than that of private buses (97.39) and the number of respondents above and below the average satisfaction score is 64 and 41 for both PATC and private buses.

TABLE 5.14

Relationship between Education and Passenger Satisfaction

Education Level	*No. of respondents*	*Satisfaction Scores*			
		PATC		*Private*	
		Mean	*S.D.*	*Mean*	*S.D.*
Primary	41	105.76	24.19	107.37	18.71
Secondary	105	100.59	21.25	97.39	25.32
College	154	97.25	19.16	95.69	23.62
Total	300	99.58	20.77	97.88	23.88

The respondents with College Education were marginally more satisfied with PATC buses than with private buses. Their average satisfaction score for the former has been 97.25 with 110 respondents above and 44 respondents below the average satisfaction score. Their average satisfaction score for private bus operation has been 95.69 with 49 respondents above and 22 below the average satisfaction score.

It is inferred that, as the level of education goes up the overall satisfaction decreases both in the case of PATC and private bus operations. The comparison of passenger satisfaction between PATC and private operation reveals that, the respondents with secondary education were more satisfied with PATC operation, followed by respondents with College Education, whereas the respondents with Primary Education were marginally more satisfied with private buses than with PATC buses.

Table 5.15 reveals that the difference in the average

TABLE 5.15

Education and Passenger Satisfaction Between PATC and Private Buses : Paired 't' Test

Education Level	*Difference*		*'t' Value*	*Significance*
	Mean	*S.D.*		
Primary	-1.6098	26.77	0.39	NS
Secondary	3.2000	26.17	1.25	NS
College	1.5584	29.57	0.65	NS

passenger satisfaction scores between PATC and private buses are not significant for all the three education groups of respondents. Therefore, the hypothesis that the highly educated passengers are more satisfied with their travel in PATC buses than in Private buses is rejected.

6. Occupation and Passenger Satisfaction

Passengers belonging to different occupations have been taken as the respondents for the study, on the premise that occupational differences will contribute to the differences in the perceptions of the individuals regarding the comforts, safety, reliability and punctuality of the buses they travel.

It is observed from Table 5.16 that the mean satisfaction score is different for respondents with different occupations. Employees in private as well as in public sector and businessmen are relatively more satisfied with PATC buses than with private buses. The respondents of other group such as executives/ professionals, students and others (which include agriculturists, labourers, self-employed and unemployed) are more satisfied with private buses than with PATC buses. However, the difference in mean satisfaction scores of the two sectors is vast for 'others' while the same is very marginal for the 'executives/ professionals' and 'students'.

Table 5.17 reveals that the difference in the average passenger satisfaction scores between PATC and private buses for the employees in government sector in significant at 5 % and that for 'Others' category is significant at 1 % level. For the rest of the occupation groups the differences are not significant. Hence, the hypothesis that the employees in government sector are more satisfied with their travel in PATC buses is accepted.

7. Income and Passenger Satisfaction

As the individual's level of income goes up, he/she prepares to pay more for better service than the individuals with less income and therefore their level of expectation with regard to comforts, safety and reliability is also high. Therefore the higher the level of income of the people, the lower they tend to be satisfied.

It is noted from the Table 5.18, that as the level of income

TABLE 5.16

Relationship between Occupation of the Respondents and Passenger Satisfaction

Occupation	*No. of respondents*	*Satisfaction Scores*			
		PATC		*Private*	
		Mean	*S.D.*	*Mean*	*S.D.*
Employees in Govt. Sector	88	96.85	21.68	89.45	25.68
Employees in Private Sector	51	104.80	19.61	100.59	19.68
Executives/ Professionals	45	92.53	17.05	93.76	21.86
Businessmen	37	108.89	22.73	104.54	26.06
Students	39	101.92	19.58	102.15	23.55
Others	40	95.95	19.41	107.28	18.88
Total	300	99.60	20.80	97.90	23.88

TABLE 5.17

Occupation and Passenger Satisfaction Between PATC and Private Buses: Paired 't' Test

Occupation	*Difference*		*'t'*	*Significance*
	Mean	*S.D.*	*Value*	
Employees in Govt. Sector	7.3977	32.06	2.16	5 % Level
Employees in Private sector	4.2157	25.55	1.18	NS
Executives/ Professionals	-1.2222	25.52	0.32	NS
Businessmen	4.3514	28.64	0.92	NS
Students	-0.2308	23.62	0.06	NS
Others	-11.3250	23.82	3.01	1 % Level

TABLE 5.18

Relation Between Monthly Income and Passenger Satisfaction

Monthly Income (Rs.)	*No. of respondents*	*Satisfaction Scores*			
		PATC		*Private*	
		Mean	*S.D.*	*Mean*	*S.D.*
Upto 1000	73	104.36	21.55	100.79	24.04
1001-3000	153	98.05	19.82	96.12	23.95
Above 3000	31	94.45	23.92	95.06	24.99
Total	257	94.41	21.02	97.32	24.10

increases, the level of satisfaction decreases. This phenomenon has been noticed for both PATC and private bus operations. The average satisfaction score of the respondents of the first group (whose monthly income is upto Rs.1000) has been 104.36. The second group of respondents whose income is between Rs. 1001 and Rs. 3000, has 98.05 as their average satisfaction score, followed by the third group whose monthly income is above Rs. 3000, with 94.45 as average satisfaction score. The number of respondents above and below the average satisfaction score has been 78 and 75 in the case of medium income group and 15 and 16 in the case of high income group.

The average satisfaction score of the respondents with regard to private buses has been 100.79 in the case of the first group, followed by the second group with 96.12 and third group with average satisfaction score of 95.06. The number of respondents above and below the average satisfaction score have been 71 and 82 for the medium group and 11 and 20 for the high income group.

It is observed that the first group of the respondents are relatively more satisfied that the other categories of respondents, followed by the second income group and the third income group. Thus it is inferred that as the level of income increases, the passenger satisfaction decreases for both PATC and private bus operations. It has also been observed that the first and the second income groups of respondents are more satisfied with

PATC buses than with private buses whereas the third income group of respondents is more satisfied with private buses than with PATC buses.

Table 5.19 reveals that the difference in the average passenger satisfaction scores between PATC and private buses are not significant for all the three income groups of respondents. Therefore, the hypothesis that the low income group of passengers are more satisfied with their travel in PATC buses than in private buses is rejected.

TABLE 5.19

Income and Passenger Satisfaction Between PATC and Private Buses: Paired 't' Test

Monthly Income (Rs.)	*Difference*		*'t' Value*	*Significance*
	Mean	*S.D.*		
Upto 1000	3.5616	29.50	1.03	NS
1001-3000	1.9281	27.84	0.86	NS
Above 3000	-0.6129	33.42	0.10	NS

8. Purpose of Travel and Passenger Satisfaction

People travel for different purposes—some travel for official purpose, some for social purpose such as attending marriages and other public functions, meetings, shopping, visiting hospitals, friends and relatives and some may take up business trips. The travel need and their expectation regarding the bus service may differ according to the purpose of travel. An attempt has been made to study the variation in passenger satisfaction owing to variation in the purpose of travel.

It has been observed from the Table 5.20 that the respondents who travel for business purpose were relatively more satisfied, than the other categories of respondents, with the operation of both PATC and private buses. Their average satisfaction score for PATC buses has been 102.52 with 24 respondents above and 20 respondents below the average satisfaction score. The average satisfaction score for private buses has been 107, which is higher than that for PATC. The number of respondents above and below the average satisfaction score have been 20 and 24 respectively.

TABLE 5.20

Relationship Between Purpose of Travel and Passenger Satisfaction

Purpose of Travel	*No. of respondents*	*Satisfaction Scores*			
		PATC		*Private*	
		Mean	*S.D.*	*Mean*	*S.D.*
Social	106	100.62	20.11	97.33	23.84
Business	44	102.52	22.90	107.00	18.40
Official	150	97.10	20.62	95.60	24.8
Total	300	99.6	20.8	97.9	23.88

The business travellers were followed by the respondents who travel for social purposes, whose average satisfaction score for PATC buses has been 100.62 and that for private buses 97.33. The number of respondents above and below the average satisfaction score for PATC buses were 58 and 48, whereas in the case of private buses, there were 52 respondents above and 54 respondents below the average satisfaction score.

The respondents who travel for official purposes were relatively less satisfied than the respondents who travel for other purposes. Their satisfaction score has been 97.10 and 95.6 for PATC buses and private buses respectively. The number of respondents above and below the average satisfaction score has been 66 and 84 for PATC operation, 69 and 81 for private bus operation.

It is inferred that the business travellers were relatively more satisfied with both the PATC and private buses, followed by passengers who travel for social purpose and official purpose. It is also noted that the business travellers are relatively more satisfied with private buses than with the PATC buses. The reason is that the business travellers find the private buses more convenient than PATC buses to carry luggage with them at concessional rates and also for sending luggage for one place to another, without anyone accompanying the luggage.

Table 5.21 reveals that the difference in the average passenger satisfaction scores between PATC and private buses are not significant for all the respondents irrespective of their purpose of travel. Therefore, the hypothesis that the passengers who travel for official purpose are more satisfied with their travel in PATC buses than in private buses is rejected.

TABLE 5.21

Purpose of Travel and Passenger Satisfaction Between PATC and Private Buses: Paired 't' Test

Purpose of Travel	*Difference*		*'t' Value*	*Significance*
	Mean	*S.D.*		
Social	2.9045	30.84	1.18	NS
Business	-4.4773	21.89	1.36	NS
Official	2.3867	30.00	0.97	NS

9. Distance Travelled and Passenger Satisfaction

The distance travelled by passengers vary. Some may travel more distance than the others. The variation in the distance travelled may lead to variation in passenger satisfaction. The more distance travellers may expect more comforts and travel facilities than the 'less distance travellers', since the 'less distance travellers' may not mind little discomforts in the service the operator provides. Hence, the level of expectation of such passengers may be less and consequently they may be more easily satisfied than the 'more distance travellers'.

It is observed from the Table 5.22 that the respondents who travel upto 500 kms on an average per month seem to be more satisfied (average satisfaction score 100.54) with PATC buses, than the other categories of passengers, followed by the respondents who travel more than 1000 kms per month with the average satisfaction score of 98.92 and respondents who travel between 501 kms and 1000 kms with average satisfaction score

TABLE 5.22

Relationship Between Average Distance Travelled and Passenger Satisfaction

Average distance travelled in a month (in kms)	*No. of respondents*	*Satisfaction Scores*			
		PATC		*Private*	
		Mean	*S.D.*	*Mean*	*S.D.*
Upto 500	157	100.54	20.85	95.20	25.8
501-1000	65	97.95	19.30	101.57	17.6
Above 1000	78	98.92	22.05	100.04	24.07
Total	3000	99.6	20.8	97.9	23.88

of 97.95. With regard to the operation of private buses, the second group of respondents are more satisfied, with average satisfaction score of 101.57, followed by the third group of respondents and first group of respondents whose average satisfaction scores are 100.04 and 95.20 respectively.

It is inferred that passengers in the first group are more satisfied with PATC operation. The second and third group of respondents are more satisfied with private buses than with PATC buses.

Table 5.23 reveals that the difference in the average passenger satisfaction scores between PATC and private buses for the respondents who travel upto 500 kms per month on an average is significant at 5% level and for other groups of respondents the differences are not significant. Therefore, the hypothesis that the less distance passengers are more satisfied with their travel in PATC buses than in private buses is accepted.

10. Frequency of Travel and Passenger Satisfaction

All the Passengers commuting in buses do not travel with uniform frequency. Some travel daily, going to offices, shops and other places of work, some do not travel daily but frequently and a few others travel occasionally. The daily travellers are more accustomed to the pleasures or otherwise of the travel

TABLE 5.23

Distance Travelled and Passenger Satisfaction Between PATC and Private Buses: Paired 't' Test

Distance Travelled (kms)	*Difference*		*'t' Value*	*Significance*
	Mean	*S.D.*		
Upto 500	5.2595	28.26	2.34	5% Level
501-1000	-3.6154	22.84	1.28	NS
Above 1000	-1.1169	30.59	0.32	NS

than the other commuters. Therefore, the satisfaction of the passengers may vary because of the differences in their frequency of travel.

In the Table 5.24, the sample respondents have been classified into three groups—(1) Daily travellers (132), (2) Frequent travellers (87), and (3) Occasional travellers (81). The satisfaction score of daily travellers of PATC buses ranges from 44 to 155, the average score is 96.85. Their satisfaction score for private buses ranges from 2 to 154, the average satisfaction score is 97.4.

The satisfaction score of the respondents who travel frequently, ranges from 65 to 158, for PATC buses with the average satisfaction score of 102.21. In the case of private buses, their

TABLE 5.24

Relationship between Frequency of Travel and Passenger Satisfaction

Purpose of Travel	*No. of respondents*	*Satisfaction Scores*			
		PATC		*Private*	
		Mean	*S.D.*	*Mean*	*S.D.*
Daily	132	96.85	21.4	97.4	25
Frequently	87	102.21	19.95	101.23	22.7
Occasionally	81	102.21	20.30	95.01	23.1
Total	300	99.6	20.8	97.9	23.88

satisfaction score ranges from 22 to 138, the average satisfaction score is 101.23, which is marginally less than the score of PATC operation.

There were 81 occasional travellers, whose satisfaction score for PATC buses ranges from 52 to 145, with an average satisfaction score of 101.21, which is higher than that for private buses. The satisfaction score of the occasional travellers for private buses ranges between 40 and 142 and the average satisfaction score is 95.01.

It is inferred that the daily travellers are more satisfied with private buses and the other travellers are more satisfied with their travel in PATC buses. Concessions enjoyed by daily travellers in some private buses like reduced fare, availability of seat or boarding and alighting at convenient places might have prompted them to be more satisfied with private buses than with PATC buses.

Table 5.25 reveals that the difference in the average passenger satisfaction scores between PATC and private buses is significant for occasional travellers at 5% level. For the daily and frequent travellers the differences are not significant. Hence, the hypothesis that the daily travellers are more satisfied with their travel in PATC buses than in private buses is rejected.

TABLE 5.25

Frequency of Travel and Passenger Satisfaction between PATC and Private Buses: Paired 't' Test

Frequency of travel	*Difference*		*'t' Value*	*Significance*
	Mean	*S.D.*		
Daily	-0.5833	32.52	0.21	NS
Frequently	0.9770	22.77	0.40	NS
Occasionally	6.1975	24.70	2.26	5 % Level

11. Owning Vehicle and Passenger Satisfaction

Passenger satisfaction in relation to their owning a vehicle has been attempted and the result is shown in Table 5.26 which reveals that the level of satisfaction of the owners of car and owners of moped has been higher for PATC buses than for private buses. It is also observed that the satisfaction level of the respondents who have on vehicle and the respondents who own scooter/motor cycle are almost the same for the PATC and private buses.

TABLE 5.26

Relationship between Owning Vehicle and Passenger Satisfaction

Place of Residence	*No. of respondents*	*Satisfaction Scores*			
		PATC		*Private*	
		Mean	*S.D.*	*Mean*	*S.D.*
Moped	28	101.79	16.9	94.93	25.50
Scooter/M. Cycle	46	99.83	22.3	98.98	24.37
Car	6	101.50	16.98	88.8	26.90
None	220	99.19	21.08	98.27	23.60
Total	300	99.6	20.8	97.9	23.88

It is inferred that all categories of respondents have been more satisfied with PATC buses. However, the difference in the satisfaction level of the respondents owning moped and respondents owning car for PATC has been significant. It is also observed that the car owners' level of satisfaction for private bus operation has been relatively less than that of all the other categories of respondents.

Table 5.27 reveals that the difference in the average passenger satisfaction scores between PATC and private buses for all the groups of respondents who own vehicle are not significant. Therefore, the hypothesis that the passengers who own vehicle are more satisfied with PATC buses than in private buses is rejected.

TABLE 5.27

Owning Vehicle and Passenger Satisfaction Between PATC and Private Buses: Paired 't' Test

Type of vehicle	*Difference*		*'t'*	*Significance*
	Mean	*S.D.*	*Value*	
Moped	6.8571	33.36	1.09	NS
Scooter/M.Cycle	0.8478	22.04	0.26	NS
Car	12.6667	28.61	1.08	NS
None	0.9227	28.40	0.48	NS

7. SUMMARY

The study on Passengers' Satisfaction is vital for any transport operator, as this would bring out the state of affairs of the service they provide to their passengers which may facilitate them to formulate their policy, rearrange their schedule and trips and other service conditions, so as to enhance the level of passenger satisfaction and thereby secure the patronage of the public at large. The study of passengers' satisfaction in this chapter reveals that the passengers are satisfied with a operation of buses by public and private sector in North Arcot Region. However, the passengers are relatively more satisfied with public sector bus operation, namely PATC, than the private sector operation. The level of passenger satisfaction with regard to the different operational aspects of PATC and private bus operation reveals that the passengers are relatively more satisfied with the 'Punctuality and Reliability' and 'Safety and Regularity' of PATC buses whereas in the case of private buses, passengers are relatively more satisfied with 'Passengers' Comfort' than that in PATC buses. As to the aspects of 'Crew behaviour' and 'Social Responsibility' the passengers are equally satisfied with both the sectors.

The study of the influence of personal factors to the differences in passenger satisfaction with PATC and private bus operation has been attempted. The study involved testing hypothesis by applying Paired 't' Test. Though only a few hypothesis formulated in this connection have been accepted, the average satisfaction score of the different factor groups have revealed certain interesting trends.

Rural respondents are more satisfied with private and urban respondents with PATC bus operation. Respondents upto 50 years are more satisfied with PATC and respondents above 50 years are equally satisfied with both the sectors. Male respondents are equally satisfied with PATC and private buses and female respondents are marginally more satisfied with PATC buses. Married respondents are equally satisfied with PATC and private buses and unmarried are relatively more satisfied with PATC buses. Respondents who travel for social and official purposes are more satisfied with PATC buses and those who travel for business purposes are more satisfied with private buses. Respondents with low level of education are satisfied with private buses and others are satisfied with PATC buses. Respondents who travel less kms per month on an average tend to be more satisfied with PATC buses whereas the respondents who travel medium distance and more distance tend to be satisfied with private bus operation.

Daily travellers are marginally more satisfied with private buses, frequent travellers are equally satisfied with both PATC and private buses and the occasional travellers are more satisfied with PATC. Respondents who own no vehicle and those who own scooter/motor cycle have the same level of satisfaction for both PATC and private buses and those who own cars are more satisfied with PATC buses followed by those who own moped.

Note and Reference

1. Bagade, M.V., 'A New look at Performance Appraisal of STUs', JMT, April 1986, Pune: CIRT, pp. 15-20.

6

Conclusion and Suggestions

1. INTRODUCTION

A growing economy needs a speedy, efficient and cheap system of transport. In a country like India, as in the case of any other developing country, the first requisite of economic development is the development of transport facilities. In the absence of adequate sophisticated modes of passenger transport such as the railways and airways, evenly catering to the needs of the people throughout the country, bus transport has become the primary mode of transport. Moreover, its ability to penetrate into hitherto inaccessible areas and the offer of a personalised service have made the bus transport an essential ingredient of common man's life.

Passenger Road Transport is a public utility service and as such it is the duty of a welfare state to provide the most economical and comfortable service to the public. By enacting the Road Transport Corporation Act (RTC Act), the Government of India recognised, as far back as in 1950, the fact that provision of passenger bus service was more desirable in the public sector than in the private sector and committed itself to a policy of nationalisation of the passenger transport services. The State Transport Undertakings (STUs) which include Road Transport Corporations formed under the RTC Act, departmental undertakings and other corporations formed under the Companies Act and the Municipalities Act, have, over the last four decades, endeavoured to fulfil the objectives set for them. The enthusiasm of the 1950s' and 1960s' in increasing state participation, however, declined in the 1970s' and the 1980s' and its share has come down to 34.2 per cent in 1989-90 from 45.2 per cent in 1980-81. Moreover, the government is of the view that the policy of nationalisation will be guided by efficiency of operation of existing undertakings and the extent to which they can provide consumer satisfaction. Hence, there is a need to evaluate the performance of the existing STUs.

The present study is an attempt in this direction. The overall objective of the study is to evaluate the performance of a State Road Transport Corporation, viz., Pattukottai Azhagiri Transport Corporation Limited (PATC). The study is both descriptive and analytical in character. The descriptive part of the study has been based on the secondary data collected from the selected unit. The analytical part of the study has been on the basis of primary data collected from the sample passengers through interview schedule. The interview schedule has been administered to study the bus usage profile of the respondents, their preference for PATC and private buses. It has been also administered to measure the level of Passenger Satisfaction (PS) with regard to the bus operations by PATC and Private sector operators in North Arcot Region. The Passenger Satisfaction Score of the individual respondents formed the basis for analysing and interpreting the PS in relation to the variables such as place of residence, age, sex, marital status, education, occupation, income, possession of vehicle, purpose of travel, distance travelled and frequency of travel.

2. PERFORMANCE OF STUs IN INDIA

As regards the performance of all STUs in India, it is satisfactory in terms of fleet utilization, capital productivity, labour productivity, conservation of fuel and quality of service. But in the sphere of financial performance, it has not been satisfactory where the losses are in the increasing order. According to the transport economists and experts including that of Planning Commission, these losses are not the sign of inefficiency of STUs but the result of the external factors such as high incidence of taxation and depreciation and low rate of fare which are beyond the control of the STUs.

3. STATE TRANSPORT UNDERTAKINGS IN TAMIL NADU

The performance of STUs in Tamil Nadu has been extremely good in respect of all the parameters of physical and operational performance and they are well above the all India STUs averages. Certain corporations are the forerunners with regard to certain performance such as fleet utilization, km efficiency, fuel conservation and bus-staff ratio. However, the financial performance has not been uniformly good.

4. PERFORMANCE OF PATC

The performance evaluation of Pattukottai Azhagiri Transport Corporation Ltd., reveals that there has been a substantial growth in the operation of its services.

1. Physical Performance

Physical performance in terms of the fleet strength, the number of routes, kilometres operated, fleet utilization, occupancy ratio, conservation of fuel have uniformly increased over the study period.

2. Quality of Service

The services offered by PATC have been well turned to meet the mobility demand of the public by offering quality service which is reflected in the decreasing number of breakdowns, accidents and public complaints.

3. Employees' Welfare

The employees' welfare too has been taken care of. There has been a well-designed incentive system for different categories of employees, which aims at motivating them for greater commitment and higher productivity.

4. Financial Performance

In the financial sphere, the performance of PATC has not been uniformly good. During the study period of eight years it has earned profit during five years to the tune of Rs.116.6 lakhs and suffered loss during three years totalling Rs. 539.9 lakhs. The reasons for such a huge loss have been, hike in the prices of fuel, tubes and tyres, mounting staff pay bills, unremunerative fare structure, heavy taxes and large provision for depreciation and in addition, bandhs and hartals which have not only taken away the revenue but also caused damages to the buses and most of these reasons are beyond the control of PATC.

5. Social Responsibility

The Social Responsibility discharged by the PATC in terms of the number of new villages connected with bus service and population benefitted has been significant. However, the concessions availed by the blind and handicapped have been in the decreasing order.

In a nutshell, the performance of PATC has been remarkable. No less a body of national standing than, the National Productivity Council, has recognised the outstanding performance of PATC and conferred the award for best performance twice consecutively during the years 1986-87 and 1987-88. The Data Envelopment Analysis also reveals that PATC has been able to generate substantial output for the resources utilised.

5. PASSENGERS' BUS USAGE

The opinion survey of the respondents as to their bus usage profile reveals that passengers are used to travel mostly by PATC buses, closely followed by private buses. The other government corporation buses have been ranked third in usage. This is in tune with the number of fleets plied in the region by each operator. However, it is interesting to note that the respondents' level of usage of buses among PATC and private varies for different groups of passengers based on their socio-economic and personal factors.

1. Respondents' Personal Factors and Bus Usage

1. Place of Residence and Bus Usage

Both the ubran and rural passengers have used PATC buses more than private buses. However, among the two groups, the urban passengers have used PATC buses relatively more than the rural passengers.

2. Age and Bus Usage

The young and middle-aged respondents have travelled more by PATC buses than by private buses. Contrarily the aged respondents have travelled more by private buses than by PATC buses.

3. Sex and Marital Status and Bus Usage

Both male and female respondents have been using PATC buses more than the private buses. However, within the group male respondents have used more of PATC buses and female respondents more of private buses. Similar usage pattern has been found in the case of married and unmarried respondents in the same order as that of males and females.

4. Education and Bus Usage

The illiterate respondents have used more of private buses than PATC buses and all the educated respondents, irrespective of their level of education, have used more of PATC buses than private buses.

5. Occupation and Bus Usage

The salaried class of the respondents have used more of PATC buses than private buses and the other category of respondents utilise both the private and PATC buses equally.

6. Income and Bus Usage

The low income group of respondents have travelled both by PATC and private buses almost equally, which the middle and high income groups of respondents are using PATC buses relatively more than private buses.

7. Purpose of Travel and Bus Usage

The respondents who travel for social purpose use PATC buses relatively more than the private buses, and respondents who travel for business purpose utilise both PATC and private buses almost equally.

8. Distance Travelled and Bus Usage

The respondents who travel more distance use both private and PATC buses equally and those who travel less distance have used PATC buses more than private buses.

9. Frequency of Travel and Bus Usage

The 'Daily Travellers' use both the private and PATC buses equally whereas the 'Frequent Travellers' use more of PATC buses than private buses. The 'Occasional Travellers' also use relatively more of PATC buses than private buses.

10. Owning Vehicle and Bus Usage

The respondents who own personal vehicles use more of PATC buses than private buses.

6. PASSENGER PREFERENCE

With regard to the preference between PATC and private buses, it has been observed that majority of the passengers have preferred PATC buses to private buses. However, the respondents' level of preference for PATC buses varies for different groups of passengers based on their Socio-economic background.

1. Respondents' Personal Factors and Preference

1. Place of Resident and Preference

It has been observed that though the urban and rural passengers have preferred PATC buses to private buses, the preference for the same was more among the urban passengers than among the rural passengers.

2. Age and Preference

Among the different age groups of respondents, the

respondents upto 55 years have preferred PATC buses more than private buses and respondents above 55 years have equal preference for PATC and private buses.

3. Sex and Marital Status and Preference

As per the sex and marital status of the respondents, the majority of the males as well as females, married and unmarried have preferred PATC buses to private buses.

4. Education and Preference

The respondents with less education have preferred private buses and respondents with more education have favoured PATC buses.

5. Occupation and Preference

The respondents in all the occupational groups preferred PATC buses more than private buses, except the respondents in the 'others' category which includes agriculturists, labourers, self-employed and unemployed. These respondents have preferred equally PATC and private buses.

6. Income and Preference

All the respondents, irrespective of their level of income, used PATC buses more. However, the degree of their preference increases as the level of income increases.

7. Purpose and Preference

The respondents who travel for social purpose have preferred PATC buses more than private buses followed by the respondents who travel mostly for 'official purpose' and 'business purpose'.

8. Distance Travelled and Preference

The respondents who travelled less and medium distance have preferred PATC buses than the respondents who travel more.

9. Frequency of Travel and Preference

In all the groups of respondents with different frequency

of travel, PATC buses are more preferred than private buses. However, as the frequency of travel increases the preference for PATC decreases and preference for private buses increases.

10. Owning Vehicle and Preference

All the respondents irrespective of their owning vehicle have preferred PATC buses over private buses, but the degree of preference marginally decreases from the passenger owning no vehicle to the owners of vehicles of higher order.

7. REASONS FOR PREFERENCE OF PATC AND PRIVATE BUSES

1. Reasons for Preferring PATC Buses

The most important reason for preferring PATC buses is the offering of 'Quick Service'. 'Availability of service at convenient place and time comes next. The third motivator for the passengers is three reasons, for which the respondents have given almost equal weight. They are 'Maintenance and Appearance of the Bus', 'Safety and Reliability' and 'Cooperative attitude of Crew members'. The rest of the reasons stated are not strong enough to attract the passengers to PATC buses, as the scores gained by such reasons are negligible.

2. Reasons for Preferring Private Buses

It is quite interesting to note that in the case of private bus operators also, respondents have stated 'Quick Service' as the foremost reason for their preference. However, the average score is less than that of PATC buses. The second rank has been accorded to the factor 'Easy to carry luggages'. 'Maintenance and appearance', 'Availability during convenient hour and time', Concessional facilities' and 'Cooperative attitude of Crew members' have been ranked next. The seventh rank has gone to 'Safety and reliability.' The last two ranks (8th and 9th) have been given to 'Other reasons' and 'Not satisfied with the operation of PATC'.

3. Comparison of Reasons for Preferring PATC and Private Buses

It is inferred that both PATC and private operators are rendering their utmost service to the public. The Private operators are small operators and ply buses mostly as shuttle services between Towns and Towns and between villages within a short distance. They are able to give more personal service to travellers, whereas the Government-owned PATC, being a big operator running mostly long-route services and working under corporate culture is able to give relatively quick and efficient service to the passengers.

8. PASSENGER SATISFACTION

1. Overall Passenger Satisfaction

The passengers are satisfied with the operation of PATC buses as well as private buses. However, the passengers' satisfaction with the operation of PATC is marginally higher than that of private bus operation in North Arcot Region.

2. Components of Passenger Satisfaction

1. Passenger Comforts

The passengers are relatively more satisfied with regard to 'Passenger Comforts' in private bus operation than with that of PATC bus operations.

2. Punctuality and Regularity

The passengers are satisfied with the 'Punctuality and Reliability' of both the operators, viz., PATC and private. However, comparison of PATC and private operators in this regard reveals that the passenger satisfaction is relatively more for PATC operations than that for private operations.

3. Safety and Reliability

The level of 'Safety and Reliability' has been higher in PATC operation than in private operation of buses.

4. Crew-Related Satisfaction

The attitude of the passengers towards the crew has been almost the same in the case of PATC buses as well as private buses. Difference in ownership has not contributed to the difference in crew-related satisfaction.

3. Respondents' Personal Factors and Passenger Satisfaction

1. Place of Residence and Passenger Satisfaction

The rural passengers are marginally less satisfied with the operation of PATC buses than with private buses. It is also revealed that the urban passengers are less satisfied with their travel in both PATC and private buses than their rural counterparts.

2. Age and Passenger Satisfaction

The respondents upto 50 years are relatively more satisfied with PATC buses, while the respondents above 50 years are equally satisfied with both PATC and private buses.

3. Sex and Passenger Satisfaction

The male respondents are more satisfied than the female respondents and their level of satisfaction is equal for both PATC as well as private bus operations. In the case of female respondents, it is inferred that they are more satisfied with PATC buses than with private buses.

4. Marital Status and Passenger Satisfaction

The satisfaction level of the married respondents is the same for private as well as PATC bus operation whereas the level of passenger satisfaction of the unmarried respondents is higher for PATC operation than that for private buses.

5. Income and Passenger Satisfaction

The low and medium income group of respondents are more satisfied with PATC buses than with private buses. The high income group of respondents are more satisfied with private operations than with PATC operations.

6. Purpose of Travel and Passenger Satisfaction

The business travellers are relatively more satisfied with both the PATC and private bus operation, than the passengers who travel for social purpose and official purpose. It is also noted that the business travellers are relatively more satisfied with private bus operation than with the PATC operation.

7. Education and Passenger Satisfaction

As the level of education goes up, the overall satisfaction decreases in the case of both PATC and private bus operations. The comparison of passenger satisfaction between PATC and private operation reveals that, the respondents with secondary education are more satisfied with PATC operation, than the respondents with college education. The respondents with primary education seem to be marginally more satisfied with private bus operation than with PATC.

8. Occupation and Passenger Satisfaction

The salaried class of employees are relatively more satisfied with PATC buses. The students, executives and professionals are almost equally satisfied with both PATC and private buses. The other categories of respondents are more satisfied with private buses than with PATC buses.

9. Distance Travelled and Passenger Satisfaction

The passengers travelling 'Less distance' are more satisfied with PATC buses and 'Medium distance' and 'More distance' travellers are more satisfied with private buses than with PATC buses.

10. Frequency of Travel and Passenger Satisfaction

The daily travellers are more satisfied with private buses and the other travellers are more satisfied with their travel in PATC buses.

11. Owning Vehicle and Passenger Satisfaction

All categories of respondents are more satisfied with PATC buses. However, the satisfaction level of the respondents, owning moped and respondents owning car, for PATC has been significant.

9. SUGGESTIONS

In this section, suggestions are made for improving the level of passenger satisfaction. These suggestions have emanated from the discussions the Researcher has held with the passenger respondents, bus crew and the officials of the transport corporation and also out of his own experience and observation.

1. Better Maintenance

The buses are cleaned before being sent out for the trip. They are not cleaned again at bus stands on the way or at the turning points except in certain towns. Such cleaning facilities have to be extended to all the places and to all the buses, especially to the night halt buses. This will enhance the satisfaction of the passengers. Otherwise, the passengers will get irritated at the first instance itself, which may lead to a chain of acts leading to further dissatisfaction. So PATC has to appoint persons to clean the buses at the turning points. If the running distance is too short, the cleaning may be done once for two or three trips. The work of cleaning of the buses can be given on contract basis.

Spare parts have to be changed immediately when they wear out. The shutters, glass panes and wipers are to be kept in working condition.

2. Spacious Leg Room

Seat space inside the bus is very limited and causes a lot of inconvenience during the travel, especially during the long journey. The leg room space is also insufficient which makes the travel irksome. These inconveniences are found in the new buses of PATC, which are built in the PATC workshop itself. So there is a need for a change in the seating arrangements of the buses of PATC so as to provide for more leg space. The overall design of the buses as adopted in Annai Sathya Transport Corporation, Dharmapuri may be adopted by PATC so as to provide for more leg space for the passengers.

3. Luggage Rules

The problem of luggage is that in determining the freight

charge as well as the allowability of certain goods, which cannot be left to the discretion of the conductors entirely, lest they may misuse it. However, the checking inspector and other authorities have to be little lenient with regard to the rules. Further, the list of freight charges for different types of goods are to be exhibited in the bus stands and in the buses as well.

4. Concession to Regular Users of PATC

Concessions in the fare may be given to the regular passengers, as such concessions are in vogue in private buses.

5. Issue of Coins

One of the main reasons for conductor-passenger confrontation is the non-availability of coins of lower denominations in issuing the ticket for the travel. Sometimes the conductor writes the balance money to be refunded to the passengers on the back of the ticket. The passenger will have to show it to the conductor and get the balance money. At times, when both the conductor and the passenger forget, it will lead to further complication. In order to reduce this problem, the conductor has to be given coins of lower denominations for atleast Rs. 20, when he starts his work.

6. Minimising the Break-downs

Steps must be taken to avoid break-down by checking thoroughly the bus before the bus is pressed into service. The report of the driver and conductor on the defects in the bus has to be attended to immediately.

7. Prompt Break-down Service

Break-down service has to be provided immediately. The next bus passing through that route has to be stopped to enable the passengers to continue their journey. The driver who does not stop the bus has to be severely dealt with. Women and children should be given preference in boarding the next available bus service to reach their destination.

Further, the passenger has to be given an option of getting refund of the fare for the remaining distance of the journey or travel by the other bus. This practice is being done in the case of private buses. At times, the passengers may opt for the first one and avail of the services of private buses also.

8. Amenities and Other Conveniences

Proper maintenance of the existing waiting-rooms in the bus stands, construction of waiting-halls and rest rooms wherever possible are suggested to offer better amenities for the passengers. Buses should be stopped for refreshment/food at PATC or government certified hotels or restaurants only. These hotels should provide both vegetarian and non-vegetarian food and also common cheap eatable items like iddlies, uppma and pongal. PATC should issue a guide on the time schedule on the various routes. The same should be printed both in Tamil and English incorporating other inter-connecting routes. Public address system should be introduced in all bus stands for announcing the departure and arrival timings of buses. The employees of PATC should use their travel privilege without inconveniencing the passengers. They should also be discouraged to stop buses at their convenient places.

9. Introduction of Express Service

The PATC runs no express buses. Of course in certain routes and services 'Point to Point' services have been introduced which do not stop in between and ply through by-pass roads, where such roads exist. Tickets for such buses are to be booked earlier by buying a token costing Re. 1. It is suggested that PATC can also contemplate running exclusive express services in the long routes. Some additional facilities such as head rest, arms rest, better cushions, drinking water and more leg room space may be provided in such express services. The additional cost incurred in providing these facilities may be recovered by charging higher fares than the usual rates, so that passengers who would like to pay more and prefer better services may be benefitted.

10. Private Buses in Long Routes

PATC and other Government Corporations alone ply their buses in the long routes in this region. Private buses operate their service in the routes with less than 75 miles. In order to create healthy competition between PATC and the private sector, private buses can also be allowed to ply buses in the long routes. However, such permits may be given to big and reputed operators in the region. Further, the transport authorities have to strictly enforce the rules with regard to overloading and deviations from the permitted routes and other malpractices.

11. Suggestion and Complaint Book

The present practice of making suggestions/complaints is to write to the Depot Manager or other official at the Divisional office/Head office. In order to gauge the opinion of the passengers and public, 'Suggestions and Complaints Book' may be kept with the time keeper in the bus stand and the address of the place has to be written in the bus. This may help the PATC to know the needs of the passengers immediately and they can act upon the same.

12. Transport Advisory Board

The Government may set up a District-level Transport Advisory Board to examine the representations on transport operations for ensuring greater efficiency. This committee may meet once in three months. The members of these committees may be drawn from businessmen, members of voluntary agencies, students, police officials, teachers and experts in transport management. This committee may deliberate upon the measures to be undertaken by the Transport Corporations to improve Passengers' Satisfaction. Besides, steps to be taken to ensure a harmonious relationship between the passengers, crew and the corporations may be discussed and recommend by this committee.

13. Proper Roads

The inadequacies of the road system are causing massive losses in the shape of fuel wastage, extra wear of tyres, frequent break-downs, low vehicle utilisation, loss of travel time and of course, the accidents. With the ever-escalating traffic, our roads require massive investment. So the government should earmark a sizable portion of transport taxes for rebuilding roads. Further, it is also suggested that instead of going for additional road network, top priority has to be given for rehabilitation and reconstruction of the existing network.

14. Regular Revision of Bus Fare

The bus fare in Tamil Nadu was low (10.5 paise per km). In the case of Andhra Pradesh it is 12.5 paise per km, Karnataka 14.2 paise per km and Kerala 13 paise per km during the year 1989-90. In fixing up the fare, the cost factor has to be taken into consideration. A standing fare revision committee must be constituted to go into the cost factor of transport operation and revise the fare at regular intervals of time.

15. Reduction in Taxes

Motor Vehicle Tax is high in Tamil Nadu. PATC has paid tax at the rate of Rs. 69,767 per bus per year. This rate is higher than the rate prevailing in other Southern States like Andhra Pradesh (Rs. 55,859) and Kerala (Rs. 23,253) in the year 1989-90. There is an immediate need to reduce the tax atleast to the level of the rate in neighbouring States.

16. Case of Subsidy

One of the reasons for the losses of STUs is operating uneconomic routes and discharging certain social obligations. As these services are being done on behalf of the welfare state, it is justifiable that the state should compensate the STUs with subsidy. The government or the respective government department can reimburse at the end of every year the actual amount of loss due to such services offered by PATC.

10. CONCLUSION

The present study is an attempt to evaluate the performance of a state-owned road transport corporation, viz., Patttukottai Azhagiri Transport Corporation Limited. The study is based on secondary data and the primary data collected through personal interviews of sample passengers in North Arcot Region. The study highlights the physical, financial, personal management and social performance of PATC and compares the level of passenger satisfaction with PATC and private buses in

North Arcot Region. The findings of this study will help the government to decide on the share of private and public sector in passenger road transport and for the overall development of Transport Corporations in Tamil Nadu. The study will also help the PATC to improve its performance. It is, therefore, earnestly hoped that the authorities will consider the suggestions recommended herewith so as to improve the efficiency of the bus service in Tamil Nadu.

11. ISSUES FOR FUTURE RESEARCH STUDIES

The following lines of research are suggested for the future researchers on Passengers Transport in Tamil Nadu.

1. An inter-firm study of working conditions, job satisfaction and involvement of crew members of public and private sector in Tamil Nadu.
2. Performance Evaluation studies of Tamil Nadu Transport Corporations with those in the neighbouring States.

The researcher presents this study with the hope that this will draw the attention of future searchers, government, transport authorities and experts, management of PATC and private operators. If the study helps them in any form, the researcher will feel that his efforts are amply rewarded.

Bibliography

A. Books

Armstrong Wright, Alan and Thiriz Sebastian, Bus Services-Reducing costs, Raising Standards, World Bank Technical Paper No. 68, 1987, Washington: The world Bank.

Arora, S.K., Economics of Management in Road Transport Industry, 1987, New Delhi: Deep & Deep Publications.

Bell, G. Bowen, P. and Fawcett, P.P., The Business of Transport, 1984, Estover: Macdonald and Evens Ltd.

Chaturvedi, T.N. (Ed.), Auditing Transport Services, 1990, New Delhi: Ashish Publishing House.

Diandas, J., Private Bus Transport in Sri Lanka—It's performance, productivity and manpower, 1988, Colombo: Friedrich-Ebert-Stiftung.

Fouracre, P.R. and Maunder, D.A.C., A Comparison of Public Transport in Three Medium sized cities in India, 1986, Pune: CIRT.

Gubbins, Edmund J., Managing Transport Corporations, 1988, London: Kogan Page.

Karnik, Ajit V., Energy in Indian Transport—The Emerging Scenario, 1989, Bombay : Himalayan Publishing House.

Khan, R.R., Transport Management, 1980, Bombay : Himalaya Publishing House.

Kulshrestha, D.K., Management of State Road Transports in India, 1989, New Delhi: Inter-India Publications.

Kulshrestha, D.K., Portrait of Road Transport Management, 1990, Jaipur: RBSA Agency.

Mathew, M.O., Rail and Road Transport in India, 1964, Calcutta: Scientific Book Agency.

Murphay, G.J. Transport and Distribution, 1972, London: Business Book.

Murthy, S.S. (Ed.), Investment and Financing in State Transport Undertakings, 1986, Hyderabad: Department of Business Management, Osmania University.

Nanjundappa, D.M. (Ed.), Transport Planning and Finance, 1973, Dharwar: Karnataka University.

Padam, Sudarsanam, Bus Transport in India—The Structure, Management and Performance of Road Transport Corporation, 1990, Delhi : Ajanta Publications (India).

Patnakar, P.G., Road Passenger Transport in India, 1985, Pune: CIRT.

Paul, W. Devore, Introduction to Transportation, (Ed.), 1983, Massachusetts : Davis Publications.

Pederson, E.O., Transport in Cities, 1980, New York: Pergamon Press Inc.

Perumalswamy, Economic Development of Tamil Nadu, 1990, New Delhi: S. Chand & Company.

Raman, A.V. (Ed.), Cost Control and Cost Reduction in STUs , 1986, Pune: CIRT.

Rao, Panduranga D., Trends in Indian Transport System—A District-wise Study, 1985, New Delhi : Inter-India Publications.

Rao, Panduranga D., Dimension of Rural Transportation, 1989, New Delhi: Inter-India Publications.

Sharma, K.K., Motar Transport in Rajasthan, 1975, New Delhi : Sterling Publishers Pvt. Ltd.

Sharma, Santosh, Productivity in Road Transport : A Study in Innovative Management, 1985, New Delhi : Association of State Road Transport Undertakings.

Singh, Mohinder and L.R. Kadiyali, Crisis in Road Transport, 1990, Delhi: Konark Publishers Pvt. Ltd.

Singh, Ratan Kumar, Road Transport and Economic Development, 1988, New Delhi : Deep & Deep Publications.

Sriramulu, C.T. *et al.*, V and J Services : a New concept in urban Transit in Madras, Dhingra, S.I. & Orpe, S.G. (Ed.),

Transport System Studies—Analysis and Policy Proceedings, The National Conference, 1989, New Delhi: Tata Mac-Graw Hill.

Subrahmanyam, P., Organisational Set-up of Road Transport, 1987, New Delhi : B.R. Publishing Corporation.

Tapade, S.R. (Ed.), Break-downs and Accidents, 1986, Pune : CIRT.

Tomazinis, Antony R., Productivity, Efficiency and Quality in Urban Transportation Systems, 1975, Lexington: University of Pensylvania.

Zehner, Rober B., Access, Travel Transportation in New Communities, 1977, Cambridge : Ballinger Publishing Corporation.

B. Journals

Bagade, M.V., "A New Look at Performance Appraisal of STUs", *Journal of Transport Management,* April 1986.

———, 'What Ails State Transport', *Journal of Transport Management,* Dec. 1990.

Chandra, Rajesh, 'Financial Performance of Delhi Transport Corporation : A Social Accounting Approach', *Nagarlok,* Jan.-Mar. 1991.

David, Maunder *et al.*, 'Matching Supply and Demand in India'a Public Transport', *Journal of Transport Management,* July 1988.

Deshmukh, A.R., 'Creative Accounting: A New Social Benefit Approach to Read the Balance Sheets of STUs: A Case of MSRTC', *Journal of Transport Management,* September 1991.

Devasahayam, M.G., 'State Transport-Making Undertakings Profitable', *Economic Times,* 2nd December 1983.

Downs, Charles, 'Private and Public Local Bus Services Compared: The case of New York City', *Transportation Quarterly,* Vol. 42, No. 4, October 1988, (553-570).

Dutta, P., 'Private Bus Options', *Journal of Transport Management,* Feb. 1991, Pune: CIRT.

Gandhi, Jegadish P., 'A Profile of Tamil Nadu Economy', *Southern Economist,* April 15, 1986.

———, 'STUs in Southern States: A Comparative Study, *Southern*

Economist, May 1, 1990.

Gandhi, Jegadish P., 'Passenger Road Transport: Privatisation a Panacea', *Financial Express*, Sept. 20, 1991.

———, 'Transport Corporations: Service leaves much to be desired', *Financial Express*, Sept. 18, 1992.

Hemsher, David A., 'Productive efficiency and ownership of urban bus services', *Transportation*, 14: 209-225 (1987).

Mahesh Chand, 'Current Issues in Public Road Transport Management', *Lok Udyog*, August 1980.

Mishra, R.K. and Nandagopal, R., 'Passenger Road Transport in India: A case study', *Yojana*, June 30, 1992.

Murthy, S.S., 'Criteria for Evaluation of STUs', *Journal of Transport Management*, 1986.

Ossewaarde, J.M., 'Public Transport—Future Perspective', *Journal of Transport Management*, Feb. 1990.

Padam, Sudarsanam, "Nationalisation of Passenger Road Transport—Looking Back and Looking Forward", *Journal of Transport Management*, November 1990.

Parmar, 'GSRTC Performance: Remedy to Recover Losses', *Economic Times*, 11th November 1988.

Patnakar, P.G., 'Quality in Road Passenger Transport', *Journal of Transport Management*, November 1986.

———, 'Energy conservation in Road Transport', *Journal of Transport Management*, March 1989, Pune: CIRT.

———, 'Modern Trends in STUs', *Journal of Transport Management*, Oct. 1989, Pune: CIRT.

Purushothaman, P.W., 'Managing State Road Transport—Andhra experience', *Commerce*, August 1-7, 1987.

Raghunathan, V. *et al.*, 'Passenger Transport in India—A customers' Perspective', *Journal of Transport Management*, September 1991.

Raman, A.V., 'Road Transport: Case against Privatisation', *Financial Express*, 10th July 1989.

———, 'The Rationale of Nationalisation of Passenger Road Transport', *Journal of Transport Management*, October 1990.

Ramanujam, K.N., 'Rural Roads for Rural Prosperity', *Kurushetra*, 35(4), January 1987.

Rao, Hanumatha Ch., 'Comparative Study of Certain Traffic

Parameters in selected STUs', *Journal of Transport Management*, February 1990.

Rao, Hanumantha Ch., 'Nationalised Passenger Road Transport in India—A Perspective', *Journal of Transport Management*, May 1990.

Rao, Rajeswar, 'Management Effectiveness in Transport Operations—A Case Study of Delhi Transport Corporation', *Lok Udyog*, July 1982.

Swaroop, Behara Anand, 'Methodologies for Augmentation of Bus service on existing routes in STUs', *Journal of Transport Management*, September 1991.

Thomas, M.K., 'Fuel Conservation: Role of Road Transport Sector', *Economic Times*, 30th May 1989.

Umrigar, F.S. *et al*., 'Exploring the scope of private participation for urban public transport supply in India', *Transport Reviews*, Vol. 9, No. 2, 1989.

Upasani, S.P., 'Is Privatisation of Transport the answer to our problem?', *Journal of Transport management*, June 1990.

Venu, S., 'Cost Benefit Analysis in the Transportation Sector', *Lok Udyog*, Volume 12, No. 6, August 1979.

Vijayakumar, K.C., "Operating Cost of Public Sector Transport Undertaking in India", *Lok Udyog*, August 1979.

C. Reports

Annual Administration Report of PATC Ltd., Vellore, 1982-83 to 1989-90.

Carpetis, S., Beenhakkar, H.L., Howe, J.D.F., The supply and Quality of Rural Transport Services in Developing Countries—A Comparative Review, World Bank Staff Working Paper No. 654, 1984, Washington: The World Bank.

Feibel Charles and Walters, A.A., Ownership and Efficiency in Urban Buses, Washington: World Bank Staff Working Paper No. 371, Feb. 1980.

Improvement in SRTUs, Report submitted to Department of Personnel and Training, Ministry of Personnel, Public Grievances and Pensions, Government of India, 1990, Pune: CIRT.

Koppelman Frank, S. and Hanser, John R., Consumer Travel Choice Behaviour: An Empirical Analysis of Destination choice for Non-grocery shopping trips, Working Paper 404-09, July 1977, Evanston: Transportation Centre, Northwestern University.

Performance of Tamil Nadu STCs (1990), Chairman's cell, Transport Department, Madras : Government of Tamil Nadu.

Proceedings of National Seminar on the Quality of State Transport Services, 1989, Pune : CIRT.

Proceedings of National Seminar on the Role of Nationalised Road Transport Undertakings, 1990, New Delhi: Association of State Road Transport Undertakings.

Reports on the Performance Statistics of STUs from 1982-83 to 1989-90, Pune: CIRT.

Reports on the Review of State Public Sector Enterprises in Tamil Nadu, 1989-90, State Bureau of Public Enterprises (Finance Department), Madras: Government of Tamil Nadu.

Walters, A.A., Cost and Scale of Bus Service, World Bank Staff Working Paper No. 325, April 1979, Washington : The World Bank.

D. Unpublished Theses

Bagade, M.V., Management Information System for Passenger Bus Transport Industry : A Special study of Maharashtra State Road Transport Corporation, (Unpublished Ph.D. Thesis), 1980, Pune: University of Pune.

Chand, Mahesh, Performance Appraisal of Public Road Transport Undertaking—with reference to K.S.R.T.C., (Unpublished Fellowship Programme Thesis), 1982, Bangalore: Indian Institute of Management.

Dixit, A Study of the Pune Municipal Transport Administration with reference to its service efficiency from 1956 Onwards, (Unpublished Ph.D. Thesis), 1972, Pune : University of Pune.

Dolas, Vijay A., Working Progress and Administration of Maharashtra State Road Transport Corporation,

(Unpublished Ph.D. Thesis), 1982, Poona : University of Poona.

Halder, Dilip Kumar, Public Undertaking in Motor Bus Transportation in the city of Calcutta : An Economic Analysis and Programming Solution, (Unpublished Ph.D. Thesis), 1969, Pune: University of Pune.

Kulkarni, S.D., Working and Problems of Passenger Road Transport in Maharashtra, (Unpublished Ph.D. Thesis), 1978, Pune : University of Pune.

Mathur, S.K., A Performance Monitoring Model for a STU, (Unpublished Fellowship Programme Thesis), 1985, Bangalore: Indian Institute of Management.

Masilamani, G.N., Passenger Satisfaction in Travelling in Cheran Transport Corporation Buses, (Unpublished M. Com., Project Report), 1980, Coimbatore : P.S.G. College of Arts and Science.

Pillai, Thalavai, Transport Corporations in Tamil Nadu—A study of performance of Pandiyan Roadways Corporation Ltd. and Cholan Roadways Corporation Ltd. (Unpublished Ph.D. Thesis), 1991, Madurai: Madurai Kamaraj University.

Vijayaraghavan, P., Determinants of Rural Travel (Unpublished Fellowship Programme Thesis), 1989, Bangalore : Indian Institute of Management.

Vijayaraghavan, T.A.S., Vehicle Schedule Planning for Urban Road Transport, (Unpublished Fellowship Programme Thesis in Management), 1989, Bangalore : Indian Institute of Management.

Index